MINISTERO PER I BENI E LE ATTIVITÀ CULTURALI
SOPRINTENDENZA ARCHEOLOGICA DI ROMA

VIA APPIA
THE TOMB OF CECILIA METELLA
AND THE CASTRUM CAETANI

D0888416

ELECTA

Cover
View of the rear
of the Tomb of Cecilia
Metella and
the *castrum Caetani*
in an etching
by G.B. Piranesi
(*Le Antichità Romane*,
III, LI, 164, 1756).

Via Appia
The Tomb of Cecilia Metella
and the *Castrum Caetani*

Edited by
Rita Paris

Texts by
Carla De Stefanis (C.D.S.)
Renato Matteucci (R.M.)
Rita Paris (R.P.)
Paola Procaccini (P.P.)
Renato Sebastiani (R.S.)

English Translation by
Richard Sadleir

Graphic Documents
Massimo Chimenti
Germano Foglia
Maria Naccarato

Photographs
Stefano Castellani
(with the exception
of historical photos or
those otherwise indicated)

© 2000 Ministero per i Beni e le Attività Culturali
Soprintendenza Archeologica di Roma
An editorial project by Electa, Milan
Elemond Editori Associati

CONTENTS

*1. Section through
the tomb in a drawing
by Pirro Ligorio,
in* Libro delle Antichità,
*XLIX, sixteenth century
(from F. Rausa, p. 45).*

THE HISTORY OF THE COMPLEX

*2. The complex seen
from San Seastiano
in an early
twentieth-century photo
(photo Alinari).*

*"On the Appian Way there still stands the tomb of the Metelli, today
popularly called the Capo di Bove, measuring about two thousand passi
in circumference, all faced with dressed white marble, of the form drawn
here...
In modern times this tomb has served as the keep of a castle erected there
by Pope Boniface VIII, as can be deduced from his arms, which he placed
all over it. And for the sake of these few houses obstructing both sides
of the Appian Way, many other sepulchres were ruined."*
(Pirro Ligorio, *Libro delle Antichità*, XLIX, sixteenth century)

At the third milestone on the Appian Way (Via Appia) stands the
monumental complex of the tomb of Cecilia Metella and the *castrum
Caetani*. The drum-shaped mausoleum, which has become the symbol of the Appian Way, is a prominent landmark visible from a dis-
tance, being built at the highest point of the road.
The geology and morphology of the site are the result of the volcanic
activity which created the Alban hills and affected an extensive area
to the south of Rome traversed by the Appian Way, creating an area
of volcanic rock known as the "Fields of Hannibal." The local lava
beds are called "Capo di Bove" ("ox-head") from the name of an estate which the lava traversed at the end of its flow. The origin of this
name is clearly the device of the carved ox skulls (*bucrania*) in the
frieze that runs round the top of the tomb.

3. The complex and the Appian Way.

4. The paving of the Appian Way in an etching by G.B. Piranesi (Le Antichità Romane, III, VII, 119, 1756).

The Appian Way follows the lava outcropping along a ridge that runs towards the city until it meets the bed of the River Almone. From here the ridge turns westward with Via delle Sette Chiese following its course.

The hill with the tomb of Cecilia Metella consists of substantial beds of siliceous lava above earlier strata of volcanic material and a ridge of tufa beds.

The siliceous lava was used for paving the road surface. Through the centuries this rock was much extolled for its fineness and durability. Each slab was dressed by hand and perfectly laid to form the surface traversed by vehicles of all sorts right down to the present. It came from quarries along the whole course of the road from Frattocchie di Marino to Rome.

Recent excavations with the purpose of restoring the road bed, where the ancient paving had not been preserved or where it was much lower than the present road level, revealed that the lava lies immediately below the asphalt surface. Clearly the lava flow raised the level of the road in this stretch above the depression where the complex of Maxentius and the basilica of San Sebastiano stand just a few dozen yards away.

Restoration of the monumental complex for the Holy Year of 2000 included excavations which simply confirmed the information we already possessed about the geology of the area. Apart from the lava beds there are also extensive areas pitted with natural cavities; hence the term *ad catacumbas* ("at the cavities") used to describe the earliest catacombs of San Sebastiano and then all the other Christian cemeteries of this type.

Palazzo Caetani was built on the lava beds, some of which were quarried. Imposing remains of these beds can still be seen in the excavated portion of the courtyard and the hypogeum (an underground vault), where the pattern of flow is clearly visible. The mausoleum, however, was built not on the lava beds but up against them: the two sides of the base facing the Appian Way and the palace are set flush with them.

This stretch of the Appian Way, like almost the whole road, presents evidence of its long history: the road itself with its Roman monuments; the fertile countryside that encouraged the erection of rural villas and farmhouses through the ages; the relics of early Christianity which prompted the erection of churches and Christian cemeteries; the mediaeval towers and castles; the spoliation of monuments and the dispersal of works of art found in excavations in the eighteenth and nineteenth centuries; the hold which the road and its monuments has had on the minds of educated men and women ever since the Renaissance; nineteenth-century restorations and urban development in the twentieth century, when exclusive residences were built here.

The Appian Way was the first great public Roman road planned for military and commercial purposes: to further the conquest of southern Italy and link Rome with the sea lanes centred on Brundisium (modern Brindisi), where the road ended. The route still exists today. This great work, celebrated by ancient writers, was undertaken in 312 BC by the censor Appius Claudius and advanced by stages with Rome's conquests: it reached first Capua and then Benevento, Taranto and Brindisi. Great care was lavished on it in both republican and imperial times.

Through the centuries the road became lined with funerary monuments, shrines and temples, villas, houses (*domus*), and various other buildings and facilities for wayfarers, whether they travelled on foot

5. A room in Palazzo Caetani during excavations, with the outcropping of lava now visible on the lower level.

or by the other forms of transport then available.

It was a common custom to erect funerary monuments along highways and many can still seen beside the course of ancient roads. The Appian Way still has many such monuments: some of them stand on public land and can be visited from the road, others on private property, while still others have been converted through the centuries into towers, farmhouses and outbuildings.

The Appian Way was greatly celebrated in ancient times, when it was called *regina viarum*. It naturally became a favoured locality for the

6. *View of a stretch of the Appian Way at the fourth milestone, by L. Canina (Gli Edifizi di Roma antica, plate XXVII, 1856).*

7. *The Appian Way and monuments at the fourth milestone after recent restoration (photo IAB).*

8. *Fantasia inspired by the monuments on the Appian Way in an etching by G.B. Piranesi (Le Antichità Romane, II, title page 1756).*

9. *Upper part of the tomb of Cecilia Metella with the frieze and inscription in an etching by G.B. Piranesi (Le Antichità Romane, III, L, 163, 1756).*

erection of sepulchres. Most of them date from late republican or imperial times (between the first–second centuries BC and the second century AD). But even in the early third century BC, not long after the road was opened, the illustrious Scipio family had built its tomb here in the stretch of the road between Piazzale Numa Pompilio and Porta San Sebastiano within the circuit of the Aurelian walls erected later, at the end of the third century AD. This provided an eminent precedent for the erection of further tombs.

The great monumental sepulchres were flanked by more modest tombs, such as the *columbarii*, vaults containing niches set on different levels which held a number of bodies and provided a burial place for people of lesser rank. Other monuments constructed to different designs stood nearby, with one, two or three levels above and below the ground. Tombs not only flanked the road but were also set further away in the countryside. They once formed an articulated and complex set of constructions, difficult to imagine from the traces that now remain but capable of firing the imagination of Giovanni Battista Piranesi in the mid-eighteenth century.

10. Sarcophagus said to be of Cecilia Metella set near the tomb in an aquatint (La Via Appia illustrata, 1794).

11. Reconstruction of the tomb in a drawing by Pirro Ligorio in Libro delle Antichità, *XLIX, sixteenth century (from F. Rausa, p. 45).*

Most of the tombs were of traditional and familiar kinds but some were quite unique, inspired by the forms of monuments from remote times and places, such as *tumuli* and pyramids. There were no restrictions in the way of those who hoped to distinguish themselves by leaving a sign of themselves or their whole family visible to passers-by through the years. The study of these funerary monuments with their carvings and inscriptions furnishes a very good idea of social life and values in Roman times.

The tomb of Cecilia Metella, one of the most imposing such monuments on the Appian Way, was erected between twenty and thirty BC during the reign of Augustus, whose mausoleum, preserved in what is now Piazza Augusto Imperatore, it resembles on a smaller scale. It was built for the Roman noblewoman Cecilia Metella, a daughter of Q. Metellus Creticus and the wife of Crassus, as revealed by an inscription on the upper part of the monument. So the size and costliness of the tomb are a tribute not only to the woman who had the honour and privilege of such a burial but above all a celebration of the glory and power of the family which erected it.

All we know about Cecilia Metella is contained in this rather laconic inscription. The lack of any specific information about her merits is surprising when we consider the stateliness of her tomb and its unusual design.

Illustrations of the tomb are often accompanied by pictures of what is called the "sarcophagus of Cecilia Metella," now preserved in the courtyard of Palazzo Farnese. But though it was found in the vicinity, it was never part of the tomb and we know nothing of the urn that must once have held her ashes.

The earliest mention of the tomb dates from 850 and is found in a document in the monastery of Subiaco known to eighteenth-century topographers. We learn that Bishop Niccolò, abbot of the monastery of Sant'Erasmo, received, in exchange for another farm, ploughland near San Sebastiano, close to the "... monumentum quod vocatur ta canetricapita. positum foris porta Appia miliare ab urbe Roma plus minus II. iuris sancte romane ecclesie" which belonged to the Holy Roman Church. The place-name has been explained in various ways: either as a distortion of the word Cretici which appears in the inscription, or more likely as a reference to the *bucrania* or carvings of ox-skulls in the frieze on the tomb.

Other mediaeval documents mention the mausoleum, always in deeds of sale of land in its vicinity. Two documents are especially significant because they describe the monument as *prezatum* and *peczutum,* meaning "pointed," an evident reference to the shape of the roof

12. *Upper part of the tomb, present state.*

13. *Map by L. Canina showing the* castrum Caetani *and* Triopion *of Herod Atticus* (La prima parte della Via Appia, *plate XVI, 1853*).

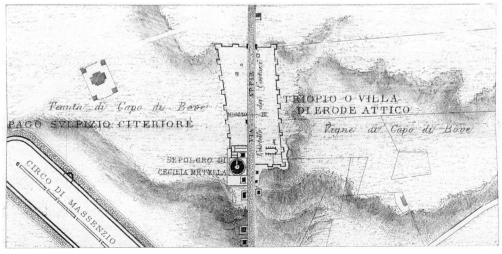

14. Valle della Caffarella and the space-called tomb of the god Redicolo in an aquatint by C. Labruzzi (La Via Appia illustrata, 1794).

15. The tomb complex with the circus, remains of the palace and the quadriporticus seen from the top of the tomb.

16. The church of San Nicola, tomb and Palazzo Caetani

before mediaeval additions converted it into a fortress.

In 1303 a castle, the *castrum Caetani*, was built up against the mausoleum, which then became the main tower of its fortifications. The result was a unique complex which is enchanting in its architectural details, glimpsed through the mullioned windows and doorways of the palace, and in the variety of its stonework

Like the most celebrated of Roman antiquities, such as the Colosseum or the Pantheon, the mausoleum, the "stern round tower of other days ... with two thousand years of ivy grown" (in Byron's poem), has inspired artists, scholars and men of letters through the centuries, and many valuable descriptions of it have survived. Numerous drawings, cross-sections, reconstructions and views of the complex, varying in their degree of fidelity, have been made from Renaissance times down to our own day. It is represented alone or sometimes in fanciful settings as a landmark of the Roman countryside or the epitome of all tombs.

In the second century BC the area around the mausoleum, which was probably not isolated in the countryside, formed part of the estate of a wealthy Athenian, Herod Atticus, by profession a rhetorician and tutor of the future emperors Marcus Aurelius and Lucius Verus. He was the husband of Annia Regilla, a Roman noblewoman of the Annii family, great landowners in this area. The estate, called Triopion and owned by Herod Atticus, now partly preserved in the Valle della Caffarella, became an immense commemorative precinct devoted to the memory of his wife who died in childbirth. It included woods, tilled fields, vineyards, olive groves, and monuments, nymphaea, pavilions, and the luxurious residential villa, all well-watered by local springs.

The features of this area are recorded in both literary sources and inscriptions carved on slabs of marble and two columns of *cipollino* stone with dedications to the divinities of the underworld that were discovered in the sixteenth century close by the tomb. They came from a monument destroyed shortly after its discovery and are now in the Farnese Collection at the National Museum in Naples.

17. Palazzo Caetani and the tomb, converted into the keep of the castle in 1303.

18. Parish church of San Nicola. The elevation on the Appian Way still contains the openings in the bell gable.

Before the construction of the *castrum*, there existed other funerary edifices close to the tomb of Cecilia Metella, as noted by Luigi Canina in his plan of the complex. This is confirmed by recent excavations inside the mediaeval palace, which have brought to light architectural structures, funerary sculptures and walls belonging to at least two such monuments.

In an area closer to the Appian Way, just before the tomb of Cecilia Metella, the emperor Maxentius in the early fourth century AD constructed an imperial complex of which impressive remains still exist. For the first time it combined a palace, the family's funerary monument, erected in honour of the emperor's son Romulus, and a circus. The vicinity of these pagan monuments to places of Christian worship, the catacombs and the basilica of San Sebastiano erected under Constantine, to some extent helped preserve them when they became ecclesiastical property together with the land they stood on.

Ecclesiastical ownership preserved this and other areas from change, keeping it as farmland with vegetable plots and vineyards until finally an economic and organisational crisis led to the dismemberment of the property and its transfer to noble families and private citizens. These large ecclesiastical estates, under papal administration, defined as *domuscultae*, fell into disrepair as the political situation deteriorated and security could no longer be guaranteed. Fortified villages began to appear: they exploited naturally sheltered positions as their defensive outworks. Set as it is on a slight rise, Capo di Bove was obviously a site highly suitable for a fortress straddling an important road like the Appian Way.

In 1302–1303 the Caetani family, in the person of Francesco Caetani, assisted by Benedetto Caetani, then Pope Boniface VIII, purchased the estate of Capo di Bove, which included the farmhouses of Capo di Bove and Capo di Vacca.

Boniface VIII also lifted a ban, imposed a few years earlier by Pope Martin IV, on purchases of land in the countryside around Rome. This gave the Caetani family a territorial ascendancy which, within a few years, extended to the whole of southern Latium, with Sermoneta, Ninfa and Norma, extending from the Volscian hills to the sea, San Felice Circeo and Astura, and part of the territory of Naples with Caserta and Fondi, and in Rome with the Torre delle Milizie until it passed to the Annibaldi family.

Their possessions included lands, farmhouses, fortresses and buildings of many different kinds in addition to the tomb of Cecilia Metella. Documents dated 12 May 1303 record the constitution of the parish church of San Nicola.

There is much debate over whether the Caetani were responsible for construction of the whole complex: the fortified village with defensive walls, dwellings (of which no trace remains), a church and a palace, as well as the alterations to the drum-shaped tomb, which was built higher and fortified by a wall with loopholes and battlements, so forming a defensive tower facing Rome. Some scholars assert that certain parts of it existed earlier. It is likely that the property already contained some buildings and defensive works; but the masonry work of the outer wall of the *castrum*, church and palace shows that the complex was all designed and built together as a unified whole.

The palace is well preserved except for the roof and floors. With its defensive wall it combines all the features of a patrician mansion with those of a fort. At least in its early years, however, it never saw military action but rather served as an emblem of the aristocratic power of the Caetani family.

The inhabitants of the *castrum*, who lived in the smaller dwellings and attended the parish church, which was not reserved for the Caetani family, worked in the nearby countryside, where agriculture had been practised since imperial times, when the Triopion estate belonged to Herod Atticus.

The church is separate from the palace and has a simple nave with a semicircular apse at the end. The facade is surmounted by a bell-gable. Only one side of this still exists, with two window openings for the bells.

The entrance was set in the side facing the Appian Way. It consisted of a portal framed by a simple marble cornice with an oculus above. Each of the longer sides is strengthened by eight buttresses that alternate with long narrow windows framed by marble cornices, partly restored in the early twentieth century. In the middle of one of these walls is another door which now gives access to the church.

The interior is rhythmically divided by the windows. Between them are corbels which once supported the diaphragm (or transverse) arches which divided the interior into seven bays. The cup-shaped corbels, made of *peperino* (a speckled volcanic tufa) and decorated with foliage, formed the imposts for the ribbing of the arches.

The simple pitched roof, which once rested on wooden beams, no longer exists but the marks of it remain on the inside of the facade. The floor was raised just above the present level, as shown by the marks along the walls. It is impossible to say what it was made of as all trace of it has disappeared.

The interior was deliberately designed to create an impression of greater breadth; this was enhanced by the light shed from the windows. However, there was no corresponding attempt to create a sense of greater depth by setting windows in the apse. The refined detail-

19. The longer side of the church of San Nicola with buttresses and windows. The entrance is now from this side.

20. Interior of San Nicola with the apse at the far end.

21. One of the corbels made of peperino *that supports the ribbing.*

22. Detail of San Nicola with the oculus and the bell-gable; clearly visible is the mark of the pitched roof and holes for the wooden beams that supported the roof.

ing and skilful dilation of the interior by trompe l'oeil effects combined with the severity of the style make San Nicola a very unusual kind of Gothic building for Rome: its affinities lie rather with the broader European context of the Cistercian abbeys and French and Angevin culture. Boniface VIII's lengthy sojourn as a cardinal in Paris must have had a marked influence on its architecture.

Church and palace are made of the same kind of masonry, known as "opera saracinesca" ("Saracen work"): rectangular blocks of tufa set in the facade and bonded with mortar. The facade and some parts of the interior were rendered, as were some rooms of the palace.

The wall surrounding the *castrum*, a rectangle of irregular dimensions (east side 241 metres, west side 228 metres, north side 96 metres, south side 98.6 metres), with nineteen defensive turrets projecting from its perimeter, actually enclosed part of the Appian Way. It had two arched gates which must have been protected by lookout towers. The impost of the gateway facing Rome still exists; it was set against the side of the mausoleum. Under the battlements along the perimeter of the outer wall, which is almost wholly preserved (parts of it are now on private property), there once ran a sentry path: the marks of the beams that supported its floor can still be seen. The mason-

ry on the outside of the *castrum* is different from that of the palace
and church, the two surviving buildings. It is less carefully built and
the tufa blocks are less regular in shape; it also contains other materials like pieces of flint, marble and brick. It has also suffered most
from alterations and repairs through the centuries. At certain points
pieces of marble and flint have been arranged to create bands of
colour.
The Caetani family kept its hold on this strategic property for only
three years. Pope Boniface VIII died in 1303, shortly after comple-
tion of the complex at Capo di Bove, and thereafter the family decayed. Though the property continued to retain the Caetani name, it
was caught up in the local tensions and struggles between the great
Roman families and passed through the hands of the Savelli, Colonna and Orsini. Here, in 1312, Henry VIII of Luxembourg, supported
by the Colonna, clashed with the Savelli and part of the *castrum* was
burnt down. This episode probably led to certain alterations in the
structure of the palace: they can be seen in the lower courtyard.
Wrested from the Savelli, the *castrum* remained in the hands of the
Colonna till 1406, when the Colonna seized this strategic fortress on
the Appian Way.
Records tell of the night spent at the *castrum* by Paolo Orsini and
Ludovico Migliorati, a nephew of Innocent VII, on their way to
Naples accompanied by a small army which found hospitality here.
Fifteenth-century records also suggest the complex was still in good
repair and functioning as a fortress.
In 1482 a Roman army under Roberto Malatesta paraded before the

23. *Detail of a window of the church with the marble cornice and brick embrasure.*

Boniface VIII

Pope Boniface VIII, Benedetto Caetani, a native of Anagni where he owned a palace, reigned from 1294 to 1303. Ambitious and power-hungry, he energetically asserted the political supremacy of the Church over all the kingdoms of the earth. One of the most hated pontiffs in history, his reputation was stained by grave crimes; charges against him include that of plotting against Celestine V, his simple-hearted predecessor, who reigned for a few months and then abdicated. Boniface was a man of powerful intellect, a scholar of philosophy and jurisprudence, and the founder of the first Roman university.

His ideas and policies earned him the hatred of leading Roman families like the Colonna, the supporters of Celestine, and above all of Philip IV ("the Fair") of France, who organised the expedition of Agnani which Boniface survived by only a month.

Dante, exiled from Florence by Boniface's intrigues, addressed words of hatred to him.

Boniface is remembered above all for the institution of the first Holy Year in 1300. He offered plenary indulgence to all who visited the basilicas of St. Peter and St. Paul within the year and the faithful came flocking to Rome in search of divine forgiveness.

In the castled city of Rome, torn by factions fighting for power and territorial domination, where many Roman buildings had been converted into fortresses (as happened to the tomb of Cecilia Metella), Boniface VIII opened up new vistas by adopting the Jewish institution of the Jubilee, which remitted all punishments (*Leviticus* 25), modifying it into a remission of all sins. "This Pope Boniface was very learned in writings (a great biblical scholar) and possessed natural shrewdness, as well as being a very clever and practical man, well-informed and possessed of a good memory. He was very haughty, proud and cruel to his enemies and adversaries, and was great-hearted and much feared by all the people, and he greatly increased the state and interests of Holy Church. Magnanimous and generous towards those who took his liking or were brave, much enamoured of the worldly pomp of his position, and very wealthy, not scrupling nor troubling his conscience about any gain that aggrandised the church and his nephews. During his reign he made cardinals of numerous friends and confidants, including two very young nephews and an uncle, and twenty bishops and archbishops from among his family and friends from the little town of Alagna, on whom he bestowed rich bishoprics." *The Cronica of Giovanni Villani*, 1322–348.

24. Outer wall of the
castrum *with two turrets
(on private land)*

castle during the war between Sixtus IV and Ferdinand I, King of
Naples.
In 1484 the Orsini, who had occupied the mausoleum of Casal Ro-
tondo, after the fifth milestone on the Appian Way, were expelled by
Pope Innocent VIII (Cybo) supported by the Colonna.
In 1493 Alfonso of Naples camped with his soldiers at Capo di Bove.
This suggests it was then a military station outside Porta Appia.
Historical records show that Capo di Bove gradually ceased to be
used as a castle and was transformed into an agricultural estate, with
the property divided between different owners. Fifteenth-century
documents describe the complex as still noteworthy and in good repair. Poggio Bracciolini's *Dialogo De Varietate Fortunae Urbis Romae*
(1447) states: "Juxta Via Appiam ad secundum lapidem, integrum vi-
di sepulcrum Q. Caeciliae Metellae."
Then began the spoliation of the buildings. In 1560 documents show
that Cardinal Ippolito d'Este rifled the tomb for marble and Roman
antiquities. In 1589 it risked demolition by Sixtus V, but the decree
was suspended after the Roman populace protested on the Capitol.
The biography of Cardinal Giannantonio Santonio states that: "The
pope was wholly intent on destroying the antiquities of Rome ... and
his purpose above all was to destroy the Septizonium, which he then
accomplished, the Velabrum (i.e. the Janus in the Forum Boarium),
and the Capo di Bove which was formerly the sepulchre of Cecilia
Metella, a unique work of the Republic..."
Changes of ownership and other events are confirmed by materials
brought to light during stratigraphic excavations, restoration and
conservation work in 1997.
In 1567 the Cenci family owned the farmhouse at Capo di Bove,
having inherited it from the De Lenis family. In 1580 part of the
property was sold to the hospital of the Santissimo Salvatore. The

25. Meet for a fox hunt attended by the Empress of Austria and held at the tomb of Cecilia Metella (1870): painting by C.M. Quaedvlieg (from P.A. De Rosa-P.E. Trastulli, La campagna romana, *Rome 1999).*

Cenci and the hospital held he farmhouse and framed the estate from 1596 till the eighteenth century. The hospital's activities as landowner are documented down to 1797, but there is no description of the other buildings: they seem to have been used as tool-sheds or cattle-sheds. Occasionally they were occupied by vagabonds.

In 1797 the ecclesiastical board sold all its property in the area to Prince Torlonia, who was buying up land for his Roma Vecchia estate, which included the villa of the Quintili.

The countryside around the mausoleum was much favoured by fox-hunters in the nineteenth century. The season ran from mid-November to mid-March and the tomb often dominated meets. An oil painting by C.M. Quaedvlieg depicts an outstanding event in the history of fox-hunting, a meet at the tomb in 1870 (and not 1869 as is sometimes written) attended by the Empress Elizabeth of Austria, affectionately called Sissi. This crowded occasion was long remembered for its vivacity and elegance.

"Fox-hunting filled Elizabeth with elation and she said that was the most unforgettable sensation in her life. The hunt met at Cecilia Metella on the morning of 16 January, a Thursday. Not a fine day for Rome, but made delightful by a wind from the north… The empress arrived at eleven at Porta San Sebastiano in a carriage, accompanied by the former King of Naples and the Count and Countess of Trani. Filippo Orsini and Marco Fiano, on horseback, in traditional red hunting coats, rode forward to meet her… After lunch they all got on horseback and the hunt began… No fox was caught… The empress had no idea of such a magical spectacle: a feast of colours, with red prevailing against the greenery of the countryside, amid small valleys, paths, flats, upland levels and small cliffs, waterways and fences, and with the Apennines all white, and snow-capped Mt. Soratte barring the plain to the north; and here and there, in the fascinating solitude, thickets, groups of ruins, and shepherds' huts. (R. de Cesare, *Roma e lo Stato del Papa*, Ch. XXI, Rome 1906).

The interest aroused by the Roman monument through the centuries unfortunately fails to be matched by complete and reliable information about its structure and the function of certain parts of it. This partly due to the lack of complete and expert excavation.

All the same records from the early nineteenth century to the early twentieth provide useful information about excavations and restoration in years. This was a period of extensive restoration of the Via Appia, culminating in the work of Luigi Canina in 1850–1853. The complex, then still partly owned by family, like the nearby complex of Maxentius, was structurally restored for the first time to repair the damage caused by the frequent removals of material from its imposing structure. The rooms of the palace were "restored" and a gate was installed to protect the complex, previously exposed to all kinds of vandalism. An exhibition of sculptures was also organised in the original gateway of the palace, over which is set a marble plaque bearing the arms of the Caetani and a *bucranium*. Shortly afterward a curved wall was erected and used to display architectural fragments and inscriptions from the funerary monuments lining the road.

In 1909–1913 Antonio Muñoz conducted the most extensive research into the site, including excavations, restoration and general improvements to the complex. He brought material that had accumulated in the two deposits of the Soprintendenza alle Belli Arti on the Via Appia and displayed them in the rooms of the palace. They include the terra-cotta monument on the left just after the intersection with Via di Tor Carbone and various other relics of monu-

26. The complex in an early twentieth-century photo.

27. Display of sculpture mounted in the nineteenth century near the entrance to Palazzo Caetani.

ments along the roadway which needed to be protected from the elements. They include a substantial number of pieces of tombs used for the construction of the fortress.

The difficulty of displaying objects of different kinds and sizes, especially fragments, led Muñoz to set the relics in brick walls of suitable sizes constructed for the purpose. All the inside walls of the palace were therefore occupied by these small displays which had at least the merit of preserving the relics from casual theft. Other relics were arranged along the tops of the walls of the monument: the marks left by the copper brackets used to fix them in place can still be seen.

The choice made today was to restore the dignity and integrity of the mediaeval masonry, which is worth studying without these distracting additions.

After complete excavation of the interiors of the palace (except for a section of the courtyard), modern paving was laid using traditional materials. This gives access to the whole area. A modern staircase leads down to excavations which have revealed the most impressive lava outcroppings. Here modern facilities have been installed.

The new structure containing the ticket booth and custodian's lodge were skilfully designed to occupy this space and the side facing the courtyard contains archaeological relics whose size and refined workmanship need to be displayed in a protected area to be fully appreciated.

28. Interiors of Palazzo Caetani with displays mounted in the early twentieth century.

29. Display on one of the walls of Palazzo Caetani in the early twentieth century.

The relics formerly exhibited in the older reconstructions and partly used to furnish various sectors of the complex have been restored and protected against the elements. They are presented here simply they have this tenuous connection with the complex, though they are actually quite extraneous to it. (R.P.)

*30. Goethe portrayed
in the Roman
countryside with
the tomb of Cecilia
Metella in the
background (K. Bennet,
1848 from J.H.W.
Tischbein, 1786)*

THE MAUSOLEUM
OF CECILIA METELLA

*31. The tomb
in a photo from the early
twentieth century
(photo Alinari).*

*"11 November 1786
Today I went to see the Nymph Egeria, then the Baths
of Caracalla and the Via Appia to view the groups of tombs
and the best preserved one of Cecilia Metella: the solidity
of its masonry is striking.
These men built for eternity and had taken everything
into account except the devastating fierceness of those who came
after them and before whom everything had to give way."*
(J.W. Goethe, *Journey to Italy*)

The imposing mass of the great funerary monument, still well preserved, stands on a slight rise and dominates the countryside.
The inscription, carved in a marble plaque set high up on the tomb
facing the road, records the name of the woman buried in the tomb:
Ceciliae Q(uinti) Cretici f(iliae) Metellae Crassi: "To Cecilia Metella,
the daughter of Quintus Metellus Creticus and wife of Crassus."
We have no information about Cecilia Metella from other sources
but the text of the inscription shows that she was allied by birth and
marriage with two of the leading families of republican Rome. The
Metelli belonged to the ancient Roman nobility and had figured in

32. The inscription at the top of the tomb of Cecilia Metella.

noteworthy episodes of the city's history. A Metellus was one of the bravest commanders during the First Punic War (264–241 BC) and at the end of the third century BC the poet Naevius was thrown into prison for attacking a member of this powerful family. Another Metellus subjugated Macedonia (148 BC) and two members of the family fought against Jugurtha (109 BC) and Cataline (62 BC). Quintus Cecilius Metellus, the father of Cecilia, was consul in 69 BC. Between 68 and 65 BC he defeated a pirate fleet and conquered Crete, which was then reduced to a Roman province: this feat won Metellus the appellative of "Creticus" and the right to celebrate a triumph at Rome. It also pitted him against Pompey in struggle for power. The Crassi were also descended from an ancient and wealthy family of the plebeian *nobilitas*, who increased their riches at the time of Sulla's proscriptions. The Crassus cited in the inscription as the Cecilia's husband was probably Marcus Licinius Crassus, the son of the famous figure of the same name mentioned by Dante for his love of gold (*Purgatorio*, XX, 116), who put down the revolt of the gladiators led by Spartacus in 72 BC; he was consul with Pompey in 70 and again in 55 BC, a member with Caesar and Pompey of the first triumvirate of 59 BC, proconsul in Syria in 54 BC, and the leader of a disastrous expedition against the Parthians which ended the year after in defeat at the battle of Carrhae and the death of Crassus himself. His son Marcus Crassus emerged among the ambitious young men who sought the honour of following Caesar in Gaul in 57–51 BC and in the same years he held the post of first quaestor and then governor of Cisalpine Gaul. The bare mention of his name in the inscription without any appellative suggests that when it was carved the triumvirate had been dissolved and the husband of Cecilia Metella was the only heir of the family who could be designated as Crassus. The choice of an elevated position for the tomb reflects a Hellenistic custom; the grandeur of its dimensions and the elegance of the facing and decorations, some of which still survive, are fitting celebrations of the glories of two illustrious families of the old ruling class, now excluded from the power struggle by the emergence of figures like Caesar and Pompey, Octavian and Antony, and seeking to affirm their importance by lavishing private wealth and refined luxury on the death of a female member of the family of no great personal merit.

In appearance the monument is much the same as in ancient times. It consists of a square base made of a concrete conglomerate incorporating splinters of flint and supporting an imposing drum-shaped tower faced with slabs of travertine. The base is about 28 metres square and was originally faced with blocks of travertine whose projection must have increased the length of each side to the canonical measurement of one hundred Roman feet (29.57 metres). Only some the heads of some of these blocks fixed in the conglomerate have been preserved, because most of them were carted away at the Renaissance to be reused. The spoliation created numerous gaps in the core of the base partly made good by modern restoration at various dates.

The diameter of the drum resting on the plinth is also the canonical measure of one hundred feet, forming a harmonious ratio with the dado of the base. It is 11 metres high (including the cornices). Most of the facing of travertine blocks is still intact: they are laid alternate-

33. The upper rim of the tomb with the frieze of festoons and bucrania (ox skulls),

ly end-on and edge-on. The difficulty of constructing such a massive work and raising blocks of such size to the extraordinary height of over 20 metres is still impressive and was only possible with the aid of advanced mechanical equipment. A very full idea of the complex system adopted can be gained from a fine engraving made in 1754 by Giovanni Battista Piranesi. It illustrates the technique of lifting and laying the blocks used to face the mausoleum, and reproduces the machinery and equipment employed with a minute analysis and great wealth of details.

The blocks were hewn to form smooth ashlar work. In particular, those laid edge-on (except the ones used to face the rear of the tomb) are dressed to imitate ashlar with their surface divided down the middle, so that the stonework looks perfectly homogeneous. High up on the front of the tomb, facing the Appian Way, is the fine marble plaque with a plain moulding round it commemorating Cecilia Metella (see p. 28).

The upper rim of the drum is decorated with a marble frieze of *bucrania* (ox-skulls) and garlands of fruits and flowers tied with ritual ribbons; above each garland is set a carved *patera umbilicata*, the metal receptacle used in ritual offerings to pour liquids on the altars. Sometimes they are replaced by a rosette. The ornaments of the frieze are thus rich in allusions to sacrifice: the ox-skulls are emblems of sacrificial animals, the garlands, ribbons and *paterae* are all part of the equipment used in the ceremonial of sacrifices. These decorative motifs were very common on votive or funerary altars; the most famous example is the frieze of *bucrania* and the festoons carved on the inner side of the enclosure of the Ara Pacis. So it is likely that the drum of the tomb was also intended to evoke the form of a circular altar (*ara*). Moreover the different degrees of finish of the stone facing suggest

34. Detail of the plinth of the tomb: the concrete core with heads of travertine blocks.

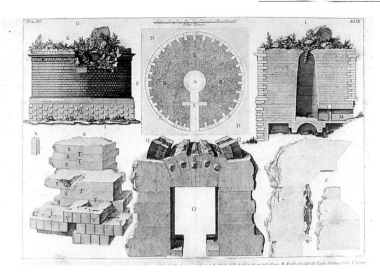

35. Elevation, plan
and section of the tomb
with details of the
constructional technique
in an etching by G.B.
Piranesi (Le Antichità
Romane, III, XLIX,
162, 1756).

36. Raising and laying
the blocks in the
mausoleum wall in an
etching by G.B. Piranesi
(Le Antichità Romane,
III, LIII, 166, 1756).

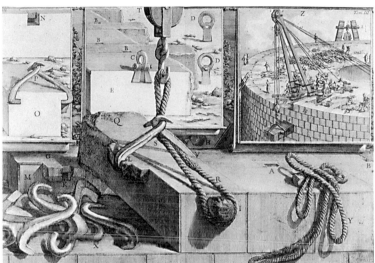

this is an object whose location, exposition and points of principal
visibility were carefully chosen, as was the case with altars, statues and
sarcophagi.
Where the frieze meets the inscription it is interrupted by a panel,
now unfortunately mutilated, which extends across two rows of the
stone facing and is carved with ornaments: a trophy flanked by two
shields surmounted by the figure of a barbarian prisoner, his hands
tied behind his back. The shields have been identified as Celtic, represented here to celebrate the military achievements of the husband
of Cecilia Metella in Caesar's service in Gaul.
The top and bottom of the drum were emphasised by imposing
travertine cornices, of which only part now remains. They indicated
the point of junction between the plinth and the drum and between
the drum and the tumulus above. A block of the upper cornice, broken into two fragments which fell from the top of the mausoleum
was brought to light in recent excavations. It can now be seen at the

37. Detail of the frieze with the trophy in its present state (G. Foglia, 1976).

38. Outline of the frieze with festoons and the trophy and prisoner at the top of the mausoleum (G. Foglia, 1976).

foot of the tomb, on the Appian Way, near the modern steps to the complex.

To the right of the inscription, about half way up the cylinder, on the facing of travertine blocks there is a small door which opens into a staircase that follows the inner curve of the mausoleum and leads to its summit. The stairs are inserted between the core of the drum and the travertine facing in which the doorway is set. Visible from the outside are the slots for the door hinges. It is not possible at present to say exactly when the door and steps were added: whether in the fourteenth century, when the Caetani converted the tomb into a defensive tower, or earlier, in Byzantine or early mediaeval times when the mausoleum was first fortified, or whether it was actually part of the original structure in Roman times. It is widely accepted that the monument had been in continuous use even before the Caetani took it over. The staircase, badly decayed by time and neglect, was restored in the twentieth century by Antonio Muñoz.

The mediaeval additions to the mausoleum have left no trace of the original roof. It was probably conical, as suggested by the description of the tomb as *monumentum peczutum*, "pointed," in a document of the late thirteenth century. In the mid-nineteenth century Luigi Canina drew a conjectural reconstruction of the monument: he imagined a conical dome faced with blocks of travertine, like the drum and plinth. Today the most commonly accepted theory, requiring to be verified by archaeological study of the summit, is that the cylinder was originally surmounted by a conical tumulus of soil and perhaps covered with vegetation; and that the tumulus was the principal element of the tomb, with the plinth and the cylindrical tower as its rich

and elegant support. The tumulus would have evoked in Roman minds the image of the archaic burial mounds, with an allusion to the family's ancient origins. This form was given its most stately and monumental expression in the mausoleum of Augustus, erected between 32 and 28 BC in the Campus Martius to hold the ashes of the prince and other members of the imperial house.

The drum of the tomb was later raised with a wall, 6.50 metres high, made of blocks of *peperino* laid using a technique known as *opera saracinesca*. This has two rows of holes for beams that once supported staging. The wall has "Ghibelline" battlements, i.e. with merlons shaped like swallow-tails. This structure, part of the alterations made when the Caetani converted the tomb into the keep of their castle, protected the sentry path around the summit. Access to the sentry path was provided by a double masonry staircase, still visible on the inside but not from below. Marble rings anchored to the battlements supported the wooden railings of the sentry path, now lost. Also connected with its defensive system was a series of loopholes and embrasures which alternate at irregular intervals in the wall of *peperino*. The loopholes are clearly visible from the outside: long narrow slits splayed on the inside to protect archers when they shot off their arrows. The embrasures form holes in the walls through which heavy projectiles, boiling oil and anything else handy could be poured on the heads of besiegers. Similar defensive structures were also installed in the rest of the *castrum*, the defensive wall and the palace.

The tall brick pinnacle which rises between the merlons on the side facing the Via Appia has nothing to do with the ancient or mediaeval structures: it is a sign of the use of the tomb as a landmark for

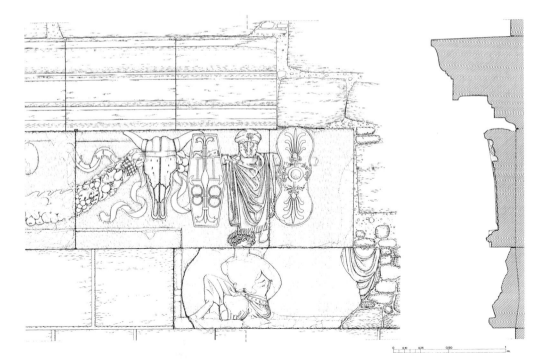

39. Marble rings for supporting wooden staging at the top of the tomb, seen through a window of Palazzo Caetani.

40. Mediaeval structures at the top of the tomb: an embrasure and a loophole.

41. Axonometric projection of the summit of the tomb with the mediaeval structures (G. Foglia, 1976).

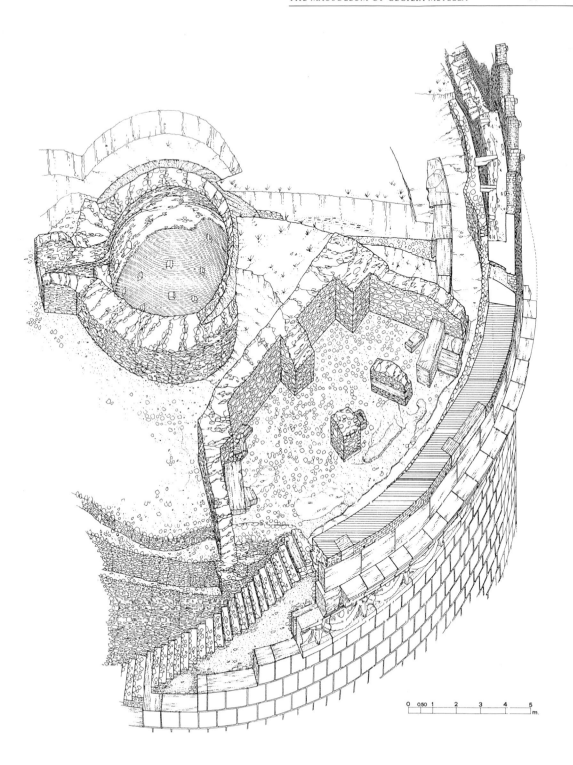

0 050 1   2   3   4   5
                                m.

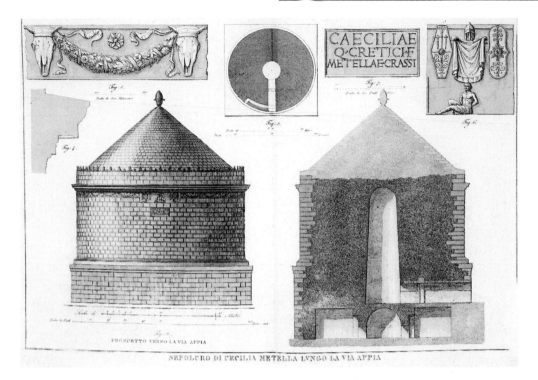

trigonometric measurements conducted in 1824 by the astronomers Conti and Richbach. Similar measurements led to the insertion of the two metal pivots that project from the facade near the pinnacle and the marble slab in the paving of the roadway level with the monument. Below it is a plaque bearing the date 1855, the year that the astronomer Father Angelo Secchi made new trigonometric measurements along the straight of the Via Appia Antica. Father Secchi's measurements are also recorded in an inscription set in the concrete core of a tomb about 500 metres away on the left-hand side of the road which served as the basis for the verification of the Italian geodetic network in 1871. This is commemorated by a plaque placed by the Istituto Geografico Militare on the same tomb.

The courtyard of the Caetani castle next to the tomb can be entered by a short flight of steps which lead through a doorway added in the nineteenth century. This provides one of the most interesting views of the monument, especially of what must have originally been its front entrance. If you look out over the modern gallery, a recent addition, before entering the tomb you can see the point where the castle and tomb join and admire the mediaeval wall of opera saracinesca made of blocks of *peperino* where it meets the core of the flint conglomerate of the Roman base. You also get a good view of the results of the excavations of 1998–1999. The south-east side of the plinth has been laid bare on the left; it looks much as it did after its spoliation in the sixteenth-century. It is the only side that has not been restored in recent times.

Clearly visible are the marks of the great blocks of travertine that once faced it as well as the heads of some blocks that are still in place.

42. Mediaeval staircase at the side of the tomb and the hall of Palazzo Caetani.

43 Reconstruction of an elevation, plan and section of the mausoleum with details of decorative elements and the inscription, by L. Canina (La prima parte della Via Appia, plate XV, 1850–1853).

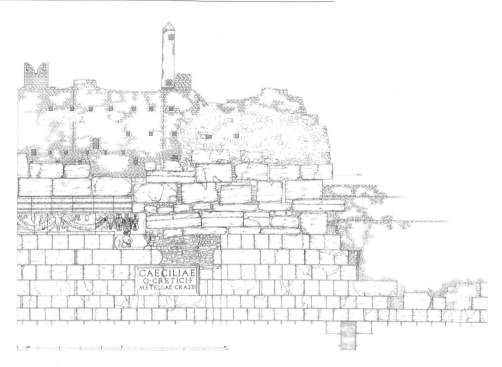

CAECILIAE
Q·CRETICI·F
METELLAE·CRASSI

44. Detail of the central elevation of the tomb with the mediaeval structures (G. Foglia, 1976).

Excavation has also brought to light the foundations of the tomb, which rest on the interesting rock formations below. Clearly visible are outcroppings of the lava flow from the Alban hills, sometimes known as "lava di Capo di Bove" from the mausoleum itself, and the tufa beds below them. The incisions in the lava, clearly man-made, are signs of the workings of an ancient quarry cut into the front of the lava beds before the tomb was built. On the right and at the far end, excavations have revealed a masonry structure connected with the castle, including a well over 12 metres deep, not yet completely excavated.

In the compact mass of the base there opens a round arch visibly restored with blocks of tufa and flint: this leads into a barrel-vaulted passageway. It is floored with a modern concrete conglomerate; the original floor must have been set lower level. The walls are faced with brickwork (*opus testaceum*), preserved only in part; the gaps in it reveal a concrete conglomerate restored on a number of occasions. After about six metres the vaulting is interrupted by a massive portal with a flat moulding of blocks of travertine. Still visible are the marks of the metal hinges which must have supported a heavy door.

The passage then leads to the circular cell of the mausoleum. The grate set in the paving near the entrance affords a glimpse of a second corridor, parallel to the first but narrower and longer, which leads to a lower level. To reach this area, not open to visitors, in the early nineteenth century Antonio Muñoz constructed a staircase leading from the courtyard of the mediaeval castle down through the base of the tomb. The original entrance to the lower corridor has never been discovered, since on the one side it leads into the cell while the opposite side was blocked by beds of pozzolana (a volcanic stone),

45. *The mediaeval structures art the summit of the tomb.*

46. *The double staircase to the sentry path at the top of the tomb.*

47. Room in the courtyard gallery courtyard revealed by recent excavations: on the left is the base of the tomb.

which Muñoz simply cut through. Nothing is known of the original paving: future excavations will seek to uncover it.

The cell, with access provided by both the upper and lower passages, is around and 6.50 metres in diameter. The walls rise up to form a cone above and an oculus at the top lets in light and air. The surface of the cone is entirely faced with *opus testaceum* of very fine quality dressed with great care. This is one of the earliest examples of brick facing known in Rome. The use of this new material, which may have had an elegant covering of marble or stucco, is a sign of the family's great wealth and of the skill of the architect in charge of work and of the artisans who executed it. This material was chosen to protect the walls from damp caused by the seepage of rainwater. The brick wall facing contains numerous slots to hold wooden beams for staging as well as what look like irregularly shaped niches of various sizes but are probably just gaps formed casually.

Lower down, level with the vaulting of the lower passageway, the cell is surrounded by a ring of blocks of stone, below which extends a level made of *opus signinum*, a layer of brick conglomerate (a compound material of lime, sand or pozzolana, and brick fragments: this compound is waterproof and its function here is to keep out seepage and damp, like the facing of *opus testaceum* on the walls. An incision made in the floor during the nineteenth-century excavations revealed an empty space below, which has now been filled in. This fact and the presence of the lower passageway have led to theories that the cell was originally articulated on two levels and that the upper level was a place of worship. Only future explorations of the interior will show how plausible this theory is.

Nothing is known of the urn which must once have held Cecilia Metella's ashes, in keeping with the custom of the time. It is conjectured that it stood at the far end and since it would almost certainly have been of rare marble was probably plundered in ancient times. It has been ascertained that the fine sarcophagus in the Palazzo Farnese, generally known as the sarcophagus of Cecilia Metella, is in fact unconnected to her, despite a tradition that it was found inside the tomb. This is clear on both stylistic and chronological grounds. The sarcophagus is trough-shaped with fluted sides and can be dated to the later second century AD, while the mausoleum, as we have seen,

48. Section of the tomb with the cell and two access passages (G. Foglia 1976).

49. The conical cell of the tomb in opus testaceum.

50. The brick conglomerate floor with a ring of stone in the cell of the tomb.

51. Section of the tomb with the sarcophagus purportedly of Cecilia Metella in an etching by P.S. Bartoli, (Gli antichi sepolcri, *plate XXXVII, 1697.*

52. Detail of a sarcophagus purportedly of Cecilia Metella in an etching by G.B. Piranesi (Le Antichità Romane, III, LII, 164, 1756).

53. View of the side of the tomb of Cecilia Metella and the castrum Caetani *in an etching by G.B. Piranesi* (Le Antichità Romane, III, LII, 164, 1756).

Spaccato dell'antecedente Sepolcro oue si di
mostrano interiormente ogni sua parte

belongs to 30–20 BC. Then we know that in the period when Cecilia Metella presumably died there is no evidence for burial of the dead
in a sarcophagus. Bodies were burnt and the ashes sealed in an urn.
So we can conjecture that the sarcophagus was found in the excavations conducted under Pope Paul III (Alessandro Farnese,
1534–1549), but not in the mausoleum, as tradition would have it
(and as is shown in an engraving of 1697 by Pietro Santi Bartoli) but
in the environs, namely in an area of the Pago Triopion estate, which
Herod Atticus dedicated after 160 AD to the cult of the memory of
his wife Annia Regilla. The sarcophagus could well be from her
sepulchre-cenotaph. (C.D.S.)

54. Rome in the Tres Riches Heures du Duc de Berry, *miniature by Paul of Limbourg and brothers (1411–1416).*

THE CASTRUM CAETANI: A MEDIAEVAL WORLD IN THE SHADOW OF THE MAUSOLEUM

55. Plan of Rome by Fra' Paolino of Venice (c. 1320).

"... and it seems that the men of that time, together with the empire lost all their intellect and art and became so ignorant that they did not even know how to fire bricks or make any other sort of ornaments. And they scraped bare the walls to remove the bricks and reduced slabs of marble into small pieces and used them to build, filling the walls with this rubble..."

It was 1519 when Raphael, famed as a painter and architect as well as superintendent of Roman antiquities, wrote these words to Pope Leo X (1513–1520). He here refers to the building technique of the Middle Ages: his words reflect the rather simplistic view, common right down to the nineteenth century, that it was a period of decline when even the craft of brick-making was forgotten.

Actually the mediaeval world was extremely complex and had close ties with the ancient Roman world from which it was descended and whose culture it transformed, adapting it to the changing eco-

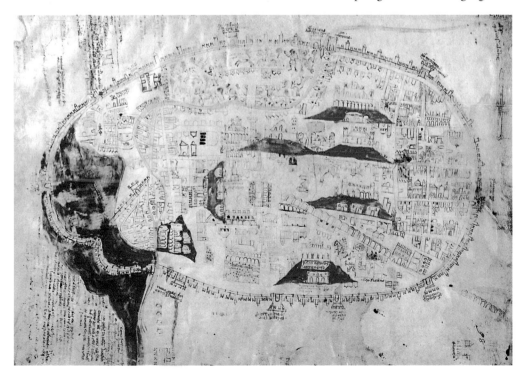

*56. Depiction
of a banquet
in the Middle Ages
(from M. Montanari,*
Storia e cultura
dei piaceri della tavola,
Bari 1989).

nomic, political and environmental conditions.

The *castrum Caetani*, which incorporated and altered the tomb of Cecilia Metella, can be seen as an emblem of this link between the two worlds, with the two monuments sharing a common destiny through the ages. Entering the complex today and finding a castle set within a defensive wall with a keep, a church and a palace is rather like travelling back in time.

In 1300 this locality was known as Capo di Bove ("ox head") clearly because of the frieze of ox skulls (*bucrania*) running round the tomb. For many years the land around the tomb was parcelled out for various uses: grazing for horses, goats and cattle, vineyards and vegetable plots, owned privately (by the Gabelluti, Del Giudice and Savelli families) or by ecclesiastical bodies (like the monasteries of San Paolo or San Balbina). Close to Rome, the area was part of the city's territory (*districtus urbis*) and naturally subject to its jurisdiction.

The land and its ownership were fragmented as was the local power structure: papacy and city fought for the upper hand, and the barons played an important role in tipping the balance one way or the other. The equilibrium between these forces began to break down when the cardinals and the pope himself, who also held the title of life senator, began to promote the social and financial ascent of their own families at the expense of weaker families and even the ecclesiastical bodies. This was because the papacy, to enforce its authority, had to try to maintain an ascendancy over both the barons and the government of the city.

It was against this background that Cardinal Benedetto Caetani, later Pope Boniface VIII (1294 to 1303), began to serve his family interests and those of the papacy by a series of purchases of land between July 1283 and May 1303. His aim was to rapidly create a fiefdom on the south side of Rome, extending from the Campania to Marittima as far as Capo di Bove. And the epitome of earthly power in that age lay in towers, keeps, castles, in short fortifications as supports to policy.

In the Middle Ages the whole population was divided into classes which were military in origin. The *milites* were either the owners of rural estates or city-dwelling aristocrats: power was closely allied with possession of land and arms.

In March 1302 Cardinal Francesco Caetani began to buy up property at Capo di Bove. One year and three days later he became the owner of the whole estate (*casalis*) and hastened to display the symbols of his power. In May 1303 he completed construction of the *castrum*. Instead of many different owners there was now a single powerful proprietor and a walled fortress that straddled the Via d'Albano

57. Rear of the tomb of Cecilia Metella and Palazzo Caetani, sited on private land.

58. Construction
of a castle in the Middle
Ages, after a fifteenth-
century miniature
(from J. Mesqui,
Less châteaux forts,
Gallimard, Paris 1995).

59. Original entrance
to Palazzo Caetani
walled up in the
nineteenth century
and studded with
sculptures form
the Appian Way.
At the top the arms
of the Caetani family.

(Appian Way). Inside the fortress we must imagine there were cattle
sheds, houses and wooden storehouses, while on the right-hand side,
as you come from Rome, you can still see the church of San Nicola,
and on the left the palace and the tomb of Cecilia Metella, now
turned into the keep of Capo di Bove.

For about fourteen months, local builders and their overseers worked
on the complex, using traditional construction methods, the technique despised by Raphael as well as many of his contemporaries.
Their work looked so rough to later observers that it was even imagined as somehow connected with the Saracen invasions of the ninth
century, as if the walls had been erected as hastily as a defence against
them, so explaining their irregularity which contrasted markedly
with ancient Roman work.

Giovanni Battista Piranesi (1720–1778) was the first to make this
mistake. He called it "Saracen work" (opera saracinesca), and the er-
ror was repeated in the following centuries, more out of habit than
from any clear awareness of the original meaning of the term. But the
mediaeval world was anything but imprecise, and this technique was
not the fruit of ignorance. It was a regional technique like the Gothic of Puglia or Venetian architecture. It was common in southern
Latium, Sabina and Tuscia.

The builders employed at Capo di Bove in 1301 were members of
the local guilds (Arti e Mestieri) and worked under the supervision

60. Perspective
view of the model
of the interiors
of Palazzo Caetani
(M. Chimenti, 1959).

of the *magistri aedificiorum urbis*, the successors to the Roman *aediles*. They favoured a quite distinctive local architectural vocabulary and style. In fact the city frowned on the craftsmen who came from outside and fostered the employment of local builders. Between the thirteenth and fourteenth centuries the defensive walls, palaces and towers were built out of squared blocks of stone. Since the concept of art in this period was strongly utilitarian, builders used whatever material came to hand. Here they used lithoid tufa, travertine, limestone and flint (siliceous lava); they also scavenged stone from earlier buildings that lay derelict and hauled blocks from working quarries.

The degree of care with which these materials were laid varies. In the *castrum Caetani* the workmanship was deliberately more careful in the palace and the church and less regular in the wall and the tower.

There were various reasons for this, including the features of the site chosen for the construction. It had many strategic advantages, firstly because the existing structures were well suited to conversion into a fort and secondly because the locality was close to stone quarries, both open diggings and tunnels, which provided material like the *peperino* of Albano (*lapis albanus*). This dark-coloured stone was used in the construction of the palace and church of San Nicola, where greater care was lavished on the architecture; this is especially true of the palace compared to the fortifications.

In 1303 the palace, erected against the tomb of Cecilia Metella, was entered by a doorway that was sealed up during restoration in the nineteenth century. It can still be seen on the Via Appia Antica next to the present entrance. Over this door can also be seen the arms in marble of the Caetani family: the shields inset with waves and an ox skull in the middle. The present entrance leads into a courtyard with the ticket office. Four doorways open off the courtyard: on the left to the tomb-tower, on the right and in front two doors lead into two ground-floor rooms of the palace, while also in front is a gallery which looks onto a fourth chamber which seems to have been a service area. This last space was probably a room adjoining the kitchen, which in castles would often lie open to a courtyard, as may have been the case here. The doorway leading into it no longer exists.

In the right-hand wall there is a well, reconstructed and restored a number of times down to the beginning of the twentieth century. It is now filled in but in the fourteenth century it must have held water, which was essential in peacetime for the builders and for everyday needs, while in wartime its absence would have meant certain death for the garrison or the surrender of the castle.

Next to the original entrance, in the right-hand corner of the courtyard, above a rather battered pillar and along some oblique slots in the walls, must have run the wooden staircase which led up to the first floor of the castle. At the end of the staircase, on the left, was the entrance to the rooms of the palace, while on the right wooden staging led to the tomb-tower of Capo di Bove. Behind a door which now opens onto a sheer drop there was once another staircase made of masonry and still in existence: it leads to the high point of the whole fortress, the summit of the tomb.

Leaving the courtyard by the right-hand door you enter the residential part of the palace with an interior bare of furnishings, lacking the central pillars of the hall, without the original floors and ceilings, without the party walls which once divided the floor into three rooms linked by two doors, whose thresholds have been found aligned with the great diaphragm arches. These would originally have been blind, not open, arches, serving to strengthen the walls. Their present appearance is due to early twentieth-century restoration by the architect Antonio Muñoz.

On the courtyard level of castles of this period there would definitely have been a kitchen, a reception hall, a guardroom and lodgings. Here as in other fortresses the guard must have had direct access to the corner turret whose purpose, together with the keep and the upper part of the castle, was to defend the palace. The soldiers had to be able to reach their posts quickly if a surprise attack was launched.

61. Rooms of Palazzo Caetani during restoration in the early twentieth century: workmen were demolishing the original infill walls of the arches that divided the ground-floor rooms (Fototeca ICCD).

62. A room in the palace: in the walls are the big holes for the beams on which rested the first floor, the marks of the roof and the numerous holes for staging.

63. Elevation of Palazzo Caetani with the corner turret, set on private land.

64. Reconstruction of the functioning of a latrine in a tower (from D. Macaulay, Naissance d'un château fort, *Cremona 1995).*

The turret forms an irregular quadrilateral and, like most defence towers, has a blank wall facing the countryside while there are two windows on the part facing inside the wall. Access to the roof was provided by portable wooden ladders and a trapdoor. The rooftop was flat so it could be used at all times. It has now been restored. On the first floor of a tower there is still a masonry seat with a shaft below which used to take the waste into an underground cesspit in the countryside. Much later niches were later set inside this shaft. Today the tower holds a small but very interesting exhibition which contains the Roman and mediaeval material found in recent excavations inside the complex.

65. *Interior of the turret with the roof recently reconstruced; the niche contained a seat for the latrine.*

66. Mullioned windows on the first floor of the palace restored in the early twentieth century.

67. Marks of the corner fireplace in a first-floor room of the palace.

68. Ground floor of the triangular chamber inserted between the curved wall of the tomb and the wall of the palace.

69. The big balcony facing the countryside seen from outside.

The palace has three levels: ground floor, first floor and second floor. The underground level which can be visited today is the result of modern alterations. Little is known at present about the original layout of the top floor, but it must have been connected with the defence of the palace. The windows on the ground and second floors are the same: either rectangular or rounded embrasures; there are also signs of the original bars, now lost.

The first floor is very different from the other two: the mullioned windows facing onto the countryside and inside the wall were refashioned in the early twentieth century to imitate those that were well preserved, an approach to restoration current in the period. These windows, like the two fireplaces of which traces remain on the walls, one at the side of the great hall and the other in the corner, at the side of the palace near the tower, are clearly not designed to bear the brunt of an attack. These features reveal affinities between the fortified structure and the "cultivated" architecture of palaces and mansions. This floor, in fact, gives the building its residential character: here the lords of the castle would sleep before the fireplaces, prob-

ably after dining in the great hall with hearth at one side. The hall could also be used when necessary as a bedroom or for public occasions, the administration of justice and the business of the fiefdom. On this same floor there is another room (visible from the courtyard) whose function is not yet known, with the only large balcony of the whole complex looking out over the countryside. The doorway on the left of the balcony leads into a triangular chamber, whose function is to link the tomb-tower with the rest of the palace. It also contains another latrine, set diametrically opposite to the one in the square turret and identical to it.

This complex, containing a residence of this kind, was, of course, meant to serve the policy of its great overlords. The palace would not have been occupied by the Caetani family themselves but by a follower trusted to hold the fortress in their name. This explains its relatively small dimensions.

As you wander about and examine the walls on the inside and outside of the palace, especially the upper parts, you realise that they are not in reality as inexpressive as they seem but tell us a lot about mediaeval life in a language all their own. All the marks visible on the buildings, like the big slots for the beams which once supported the floor or the smaller ones for the scaffolding, reveal the way the *castrum* was built in those fourteen months and how many people worked on it.

Work started in 1302 on a number of different structures with a master builder (*magister*) to direct and co-ordinate the host of workmen

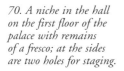

70. A niche in the hall on the first floor of the palace with remains of a fresco; at the sides are two holes for staging.

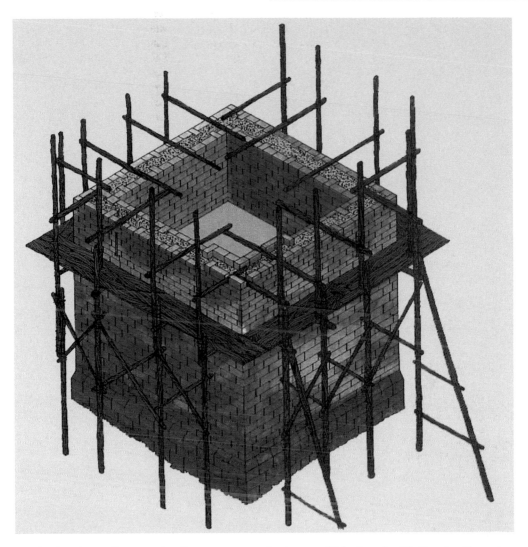

involved. The walls were the first part erected. A row of blocks of stone was laid to mark the inner and outer side of the wall, and the cavity between them was filled up with mortar. Then small irregular fragments of stone and brick were carefully inserted to fill the fissures between the blocks. Trapezoidal blocks of *peperino* ensured greater cohesion with the core of mortar. In this way the construction rose row after row, with the scaffolding and wooden catwalks rising to keep pace with it. Signs of them remain in the holes, open or partly blocked up, in the bare walls. The scaffolding was designed to enable the builders to work comfortably standing erect. Mortar was also smeared on the blocks of stone to make good their irregularities, as can still be seen.

The defensive function of the complex as a whole meant that only the residential part allowed the magister or architect or some scope for adding architectural or artistic touches, which recall features of the Cistercian architecture of the same period: these were mainly

71. Drawing illustrating the technique of building a wall in opera saracinesca *(from D. Fironai,* Tecniche costruttive murarie medievali – il Lazio meridionale, Rome 1996).

functional details to improve the ventilation and illumination of large spaces. They also appear outside the palace in the nave of the church of San Nicola.

San Nicola can be seen as a late example of Cistercian architecture, a style which was born in France and spread through Europe with the abbeys and the religious ideals of the Cistercian monks. The order founded numerous abbeys in Italy from the twelfth century on. The Roman builders were clearly familiar with the new ideas and style which, as always, they adapted to the local and to the materials locally available. Hence the various features typical of the Cistercian style: buttresses, pointed windows and the oculus set at the very centre above the doorway. The sobriety of the interior, bare of decoration, reflects the religious thinking and austere ideals of the Cistercians, who returned to the strict Benedictine rule that nothing should distract the monks' minds from prayer. A document of 1303 shows that the church of San Nicola had parochial rights (*jura parrochialia*). This proves it was not merely the Caetani family chapel but cared for the spiritual needs of all the people who lived in the *castrum* and worked the land around it for their feudal overlords.

If you walk along the remains of the wall behind the church of San Nicola or glance at the top of the tomb, you can see the natural materials and the morphology of the terrain on which the fortress was erected. The estate supplied the construction materials, while projections, platforms, and irregularities of the terrain were exploited for defensive and constructional purposes. And so the presence of the ancient flint quarry (the stone is a siliceous lava), the many funerary monuments of marble, travertine, and brick, the pozzolana quarries

72. Exterior of the church of San Nicola with the apse.

73. Interior of the church: in the background the side with the entrance surmounted by the remains of the bell gable and the door walled up in the early twentieth century.

74. Outer wall of the castle with two of the towers ranged along its perimeter, now in private grounds.

75. Depiction of a siege of a castle in the Middle Ages, after a manuscript (from J. Mesqui, Les châteaux forts, Gallimard, Paris 1995).

lower down, as well as the entire tower-shaped tomb of Cecilia Metella were of crucial importance in the economy of this mediaeval building site. At least two of the funerary monuments close by the mausoleum were destroyed for building materials, shaped and used together with the lava in the construction of the defensive wall.

By 1303 a quadrilateral outer wall had been erected with numerous turrets. Two of the main gates stood on the Appian Way: the Rome gate, protected by the turret of Capo di Bove and the Alban gate. There were also two posterns in the longer sides. The towers set in the perimeter of the wall and still partly visible were carefully positioned so that, at least in theory, they were never further apart than twice the range of the weapons (bows and cross-bows) used by the garrison, who could thus strike at the flanks of an attacker. These towers are of the type known as *scudate* or shield towers, closed only on the outer side; the inner side is completely open above the line of the walls to prevent the enemy from taking them and transforming them into a bridgehead.

The outer wall, castle and keep have pointed merlons at the top, conventionally described, though for no good historical reason, as "Ghibelline" battlements. The merlons and the parapet create a system of alternating open and closed spaces providing shelter for the defenders while they awaited an opportunity to use their weapons. There were marble rings attached to the battlements used to secure makeshift wooden structures to shelter the defenders from the sun and rain or a raised walkway to enable them to move easily. This was the more necessary because the thickness of the walls is barely sufficient for a sentry path but inadequate for mounting a full-scale

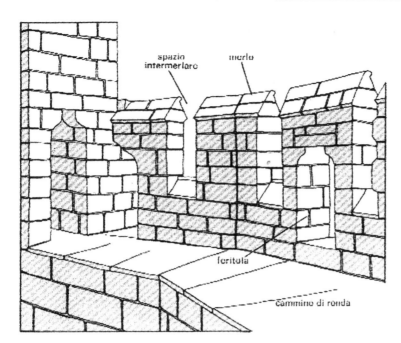

spazio
intermerlare

merlo

feritola

cammino di ronda

*76. Reconstruction
of the mediaeval
battlements and the
sentry path
(from J. Hogg,* Storia
delle fortificazioni,
Novara, 1982).

*77. Reconstruction
of the wooden staging
(from J. Hogg,* Storia
delle fortificazioni,
Novara, 1982).

78. View of the geometrical model of Palazzo Caetani; in the foreground, part of the summit of the tomb (M. Chimenti, 1999).

defence. This would involve numerous soldiers using bows or cross-bows while other soldiers dropped heavy stones or poured boiling liquids onto the heads of the attackers through embrasures provided for the purpose. The best place to position the latter was clearly the tower of Capo di Bove, where two can still be seen.

As the imposing keep of the *castrum Caetani*, in the fourteenth century the tower faced towards Rome, the symbol of a power that was approaching dangerously close to the city and feared above all by the Orsini and Colonna families.

Boniface VIII's policy of personal aggrandisement was quite outrageous but it came to an end with his death in 1303. After this the fortress passed through various hands, gradually losing its original significance as the embodiment of the power of a family controlling an immense territory.

The crises of the papacy and its transfer to Avignon in Provence (1309–1376) were signs of the recrudescence of popular municipal power in Rome. Some of the baronial families of the city, like the Orsini, the Colonna and the Savelli, preserved and in the pope's absence probably enlarged the prerogatives they had won in the previous century. Others, like the Caetani, disappeared from Latium and

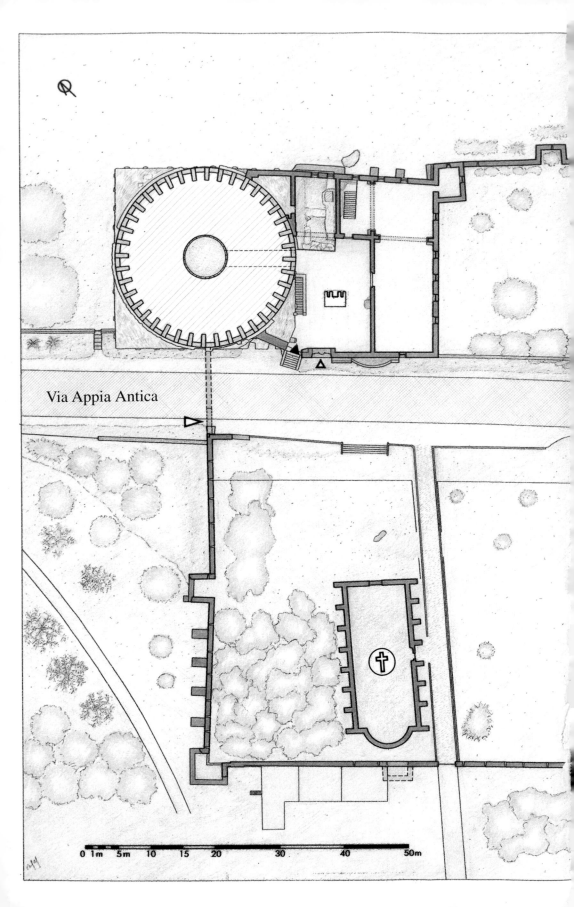

Via Appia Antica

0 1m 5m 10 15 20 30 40 50m

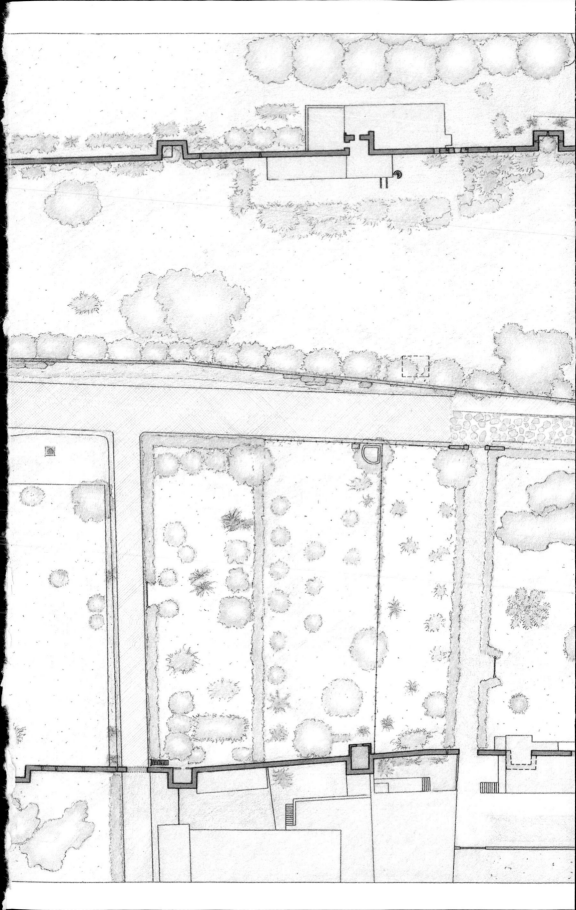

their possessions in Rome were gradually dismantled. An atmosphere of danger and decadence began to spread which soon led to the dereliction of the castle and the whole area.

When the popes returned to Rome it was of little use for the papal state to possess strategic fortifications against the anarchy created by the new baronial order, with the violence of the *milites*. As late as the fifteenth century castles were two-edged weapons because they could easily become centres of rebellion, depending on who held them. In the course of the century the lands of the *castrum* continued to change hands; the palace was briefly occupied by different owners and at times even uninhabited (1484). The Roman tomb once more became the dominant feature: while builders came scavenging for stone and applications were made for permission—regularly refused by the municipality of Rome—to despoil it, with quarrels over the ownership of the castle (in the early seventeenth century), the history of the tomb gradually became separate once more from that of the palace.

So it happened that eventually even poets and writers fascinated by the area could not resist speaking of it, from Byron (1788–1824), who described it as "a stern round tower," to Goethe (1749–1832), who saw it as embodying the greatness of the Roman gens who "built for eternity," down to the present, when we enter the imposing tomb and explore what lies in its shadow.

In reality the bonds between what are in our own day considered two separate monuments are still very close. The castrum, at the start of its history, almost certainly saved the mausoleum of Cecilia Metella from destruction, given the lot that befell many other sepulchres along the Appian Way: at the end of its history the stateliness of the Roman monument has merely returned this favour to the castle.

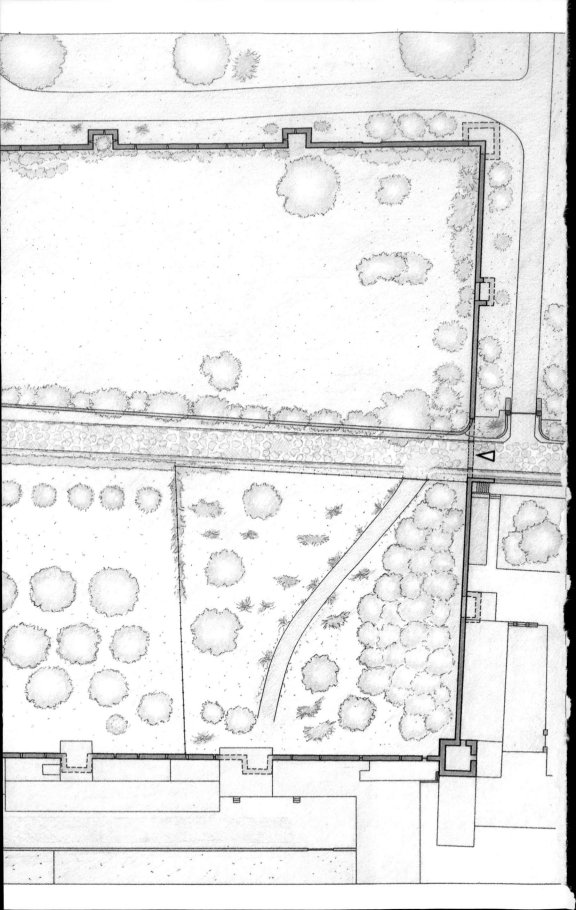

Sepulchre of Cecilia Metella

 Castrum Caetani

 Present entrance to the castle

 Mediaeval entrance

 Church of San Nicola di Bari

 Roman course of the Via Appia

 Defensive wall of the castrum

 Tower destroyed or incorporated in the modern building

 North portal of the castrum, now lost. The remains of the right-hand jamb can be seen

 South portal now lost

 Loopholes

Table I
Plan
and reconstruction
of the castrum
Caetani
(M. Naccarato)

 Modern private buildings

MATERIALS FOR A MUSEUM OF THE APPIAN WAY IN PALAZZO CAETANI

79. Funerary relief with two figures and an inscription

80. Original entrance to Palazzo Caetani walled up and decorated with sculptures.

Even in the Middle Ages the troubled history of this monumental complex led to the destruction of the surviving archaeological relics in the area. However the rediscovery and reclamation of the Appian Way in the earlier nineteenth century under Pius VII and Pius IX initiated a period of outstanding archaeological excavations and new finds. The scholars who supervised the intense studies fostered by the popes introduced what is now an established principle: that archaeological relics should not be removed to big museums, already rich in exhibits, even less to their reserve collections, but displayed in their original setting so as to reveal their close links with it.

These ideals led to the construction of small masonry walls on the Appian Way to hold the marble fragments recovered in excavations; the original doorway of Palazzo Caetani was also walled up and used to display some of the more significant relics found in the tomb. These include a male statue from the reign of Hadrian, which probably represented an emperor clad in a short cloak, the chlamys, and the lorica, the Roman breastplate; a draped female figure of the second century AD in a chiton—a light Greek garment—clasped at the waist by a broad fascia and with a himation wrapped around it; a

fragment of a sarcophagus, dating from the second century AD, depicting an cupid holding a clipeus.

Further discoveries of sculptural, architectural and epigraphic fragments created the need for a larger exhibition space at the front of the castle. A wall to the right of the filled-in doorway was chosen for the display of an inscription of the *tribunus militum Q. Granius Labeo* (late first century BC or the early first century AD), and another of the *praefectus equitum T. Crustidius Briso* (first century AD). The latter comes from a circular monument as is shown by the fragments of a cornice with a plain moulding displayed in the wall below it.

It was only in the twentieth century it was decided to turn the tomb of Cecilia Metella and the Caetani castle into the premises of an archaeological collection proper. In 1909–1913 Antonio Muñoz, as inspector of the Regia Sovrintendenza ai Monumenti, decided to mount a small "Antiquarium" in the courtyard and interiors of Palazzo Caetani, intending that it should eventually grow into a museum of the Appian Way.

Muñoz undertook to display for the first time the wealth of archaeological remains from the nineteenth-century excavations, then deposited without any plan or indication of provenance in two tombs near the Appian Way. The material comprised inscriptions, capitals, *antifixae*, architraves, plinths, corbels, friezes, reliefs, sarcophagi, and free-standing sculptures of various sizes. The problem of how to display these materials was solved by fastening them to the existing walls of the complex, while smaller pieces, which risked being pilfered, were inserted in low bricks walls specially built for the purpose. Large items were also treated in this way if they required a support. The arrangement of the material was decorative rather than systematic, in keeping within the antiquarian taste of the period. Consequently the severe masonry work in *opera saracinesca* of the castle was enlivened with friezes, heads, busts, reliefs and inscriptions without any con-

81. Rooms of Palazzo Caetani with the early twentieth-century display.

cern for the structural function of the fragments. In some cases they were arranged in bold patterns with an urn set above a plinth or a capital, favouring displays that set off particularly fine pieces while neglecting comprehension of the historical and archaeological significance of each item. They formed a striking decor for the interior of the castle and provide interesting testimony to the taste of the period.

The care taken to anchor the pieces to the walls failed to prevent numerous thefts. Some of the more valuable items were moved for safe-

82, 83. Arrangement of sculptures in the early twentieth-century display.

keeping to the Museo Nazionale Romano. This impoverishment of the collection there has been followed recently by a new phase of expansion. The monument, now fitted with modern security systems, houses not just items turned up in recent excavations but also other material previously stored along the Via Appia. Unfortunately, once again these transfers were not properly documented, so that it is not always possible to determine the provenance of the relics or distinguish new finds from old.

The work carried out in 1998–1999 also raised the need to reorganise the old display by the freeing the castle walls from the exhibits and demolishing the brick walls. This is essential to the conservation of the exhibits, which suffered from corrosion by damp, dust and rainwater. It will also liberate the mediaeval walls from the metal brackets and pieces of mortar used to support the exhibits. All the items chosen for the new exhibition were restored if they had suffered damage from wind, rain, dust or lichens and they were arranged, as far as possible, by period and type, while keeping together the items found at Forte Appio, the only nucleus of material whose provenance was reliably known. All the material displayed is known to have come from the Appian Way (there is sometimes documentary evidence of this) and to belong to funerary monuments from between the second century BC and the fourth century AD.

The exhibits represent the main types of funerary monuments and objects: urns of various forms which contained the ashes of the deceased, sarcophagi in which the bodies were laid for inhumation, especially common from the second century AD, *cippi* (pillars) used to mark underground burials and bearing the name of the departed, inscriptions, reliefs with figurative or vegetable decorations, statues and portraits from the facades of funerary monuments. The Antiquarium thus provides an introduction to a tour of the Appian Way and makes it possible to reconstruct, at least in part, the appearance of the road in Roman times.

The courtyard retains its previous function as a museum of inscribed stone slabs and tablets, but a number of fine sculptures and reliefs from the fronts of funerary monuments have been added. The exhibits have been increased by some notable items brought to light during restoration of the Appian Way in 1998–1999.

On the left of the entrance are two reliefs with lictorial fasciae, both from the first century AD. Carvings of fasciae on the main facades of sepulchres signified that the deceased held the rank of magistrate and derived from the custom of hanging the lictor's fasciae in the atrium of the home. The great slab of travertine opposite the gate bears a metrical inscription in Saturnian verses which takes the customary form of a dialogue with a passer-by. The slab was part of a funerary monument dedicated one Marcus Cecilius and dates from the first century BC.

The new ticket office contains a small showcase with a display of exhibits requiring protection because of their size and form. Some of the more interesting are described here. The two fragments of a relief of tragic masks were part of a large slab with several rows of decoration. They may well come from a tomb; masks were commonly used as funerary symbols for their decorative value, symbolism (the pow-

ers attributed to such masks), and their association with the god Dionysus, connected with the immortality of the soul. The front of the fluted sarcophagus with a lion protome dates from the mid-second century. This is a common decorative scheme on sarcophagi: they usually had two lions whose jaws held a ring, lost in this example. The thick locks of the mane flutter about the lion's head but the carving is restrained compared with many later examples.

A fragment contains a carving (second century AD) of Hermes, probably as Psychopomp, who accompanied the souls of the dead to the underworld. Only part of the torso remains, with the mantle slung over one shoulder and part of the caduceus on his right arm. The lid of an urn, particularly elegant and refined, in the form of a

84, 85. Reliefs with theatrical masks.

86. Front of a sarcophagus with lion relief.

87. *Lid of an urn.*
88. *Head of a man.*

small tympanum is decorated with a *gorgoneion* and vegetable motifs. The workmanship of the relief and type of ornament suggest it is from the second century BC.

The head of a man is an interesting example of a realistic Roman funerary portrait and probably dates from the second century BC.

The frieze with a *bucranium* dating from the first century is common decorative feature of funerary monuments, of which the mausoleum of Cecilia Metella is the most famous example.

A terra-cotta panel depicts panthers flanking a crater: these motifs are both closely linked to the cult of Dionysus. Dating from the first century BC, it was found in the recent excavations in the Torricola area near the Appian Way

The courtyard contains a collection of materials all known to share the same provenance. This is a group of inscriptions, most of them on pillars but also other materials, discovered in 1878 during excavations at Forte Appio (at the fourth mile of the Appian Way). This brought to light an extensive area of sepulchral inscriptions. The pillars of *peperino* and travertine served to mark an underground burial or the boundaries of sepulchral precincts or buildings. The two largest (first century BC) are made of *peperino* and toward an oriental name of Thracian origin, M. Papinius Zibax. They have a large hole in the top, originally embedded in the ground, through which was passed a log of wood to fix them securely in place. Dating from the first century AD are two white marble urns and a funerary urn containing two compartments, with the names of two freedmen, Papinia Rhodine and Marcus Papinius Dionisius, inscribed within a *tabula ansata*. Also interesting is a white marble ara with an inscription of the imperial freedman Sabinus (second century AD); its sides bear two sacred symbols, the urceus and the patera, and at the top a cavity to hold the votive of the dead. A cippus from the fourth century AD contains a metrical inscription in Greek by Pontianus, a foreigner born at Amastri on the Pontus in Asia Minor. The rear of this cippus depicts a *lanthulum*.

The great hall of the castle contains a display of statuary stones and architectural decorations from these monuments. Immediately before

pp. Cippus with Greek
inscription
and carvings.

90. Funerary statue of a male figure wearing a toga.

*91. Funerary statue
of a draped female figure.*

you on entering the hall are a number of male figures in togas and a draped female figure, life-size or slightly larger, all from funerary monuments found on the Appian Way in modern or earlier excavations. In republican times the custom spread of erecting funerary statues to the deceased, usually represented wearing the toga, the traditional woollen garment, worn over a plain tunic whose simplicity expressed the values and political structure of Roman society. Until late antiquity the toga, though confined to formal occasions, remained a symbol of official privileges bound up with age, sex and social class. Boys wore the *toga praetexta*, edged with purple, and only when they attained manhood could they don the white *toga virilis*.

Along the wall to the left of the entrance are a number of Ionic capitals set on two cornices from a single monument with a round plan. They were found during recent excavations in the palace. The Ionic capital originated in Asia Minor and acquired its canonical form in Greece in the fifth century BC: with a square abacus and two reels at the sides, and a second type with four faces, diagonal volutes and without reels. The two models spread to Rome respectively from the third and second centuries BC. They continued to be used all through imperial times, with minor modifications into a more sculptural, a chiaroscuro, and a linear form.

To the right of the door is a group of capitals of different sizes in the Corinthian style or modified forms of it. The Corinthian capital was brought to Rome by Greek craftsmen in the second century BC. The modified form, with volutes of vegetation, was particularly common from Augustan to Flavian times, and continued to in use till the fourth century BC.

Along the walls the exhibits include numerous architectural elements which testify to the richness and variety of the decorations on funerary monuments, of which only the concrete cores usually now survive, stripped of their facing. The items include a cornice with ovo-

92. Ionic Capital.

93. *Corinthian capital.*

lo, astragal, and dentil mouldings from a large circular sepulchre, a fragment of frieze with a garland (a recent find), and a section of trabeation richly decorated with acanthus leaves and wavelets.

The passage between this room and the following one contains a display of funerary urns from the first century AD, some of them bearing the name of the deceased inscribed on one of the handles or the lid. Along the right-hand wall of the following room are a square urn with a *tabula ansata* on the front which must have borne the name of the deceased, an urn with two compartments for the ashes of two people; its front is divided by pillars decorated with a vine shoot (second or third century AD).

A simple sarcophagus (second century AD) held the body of the freedwoman Aelia Zosime: its only decorative feature is an elegant *tabula ansata* which encloses the inscription, carved in large, regular deeply cut letters.

In the middle of the end wall is a large funerary relief consisting of a number of slabs of limestone dating from republican times (second–first century BC). It represents two male figures: the one on the left, only partly preserved, is dressed in a tunic and palium and the hair is dressed with a wig; the one on the left is much smaller, probably representing a boy, and similarly dressed, and holds the hand of a third figure on its right, of which only the hand remains. Over the boy's head, is an inscription set in a shallow square: *M(anius) Tettius M(ani) filius*. At the top it preserves a lead bracket.

Next to it is a relief with a trophy of arms from the front of a funerary monument, perhaps of someone distinguished for military

94. *Architectural element from a circular funerary monument.*

95. *Frieze with garland from a circular funerary monument.*

achievements. The trophy consists of a shield decorated with lanceolate leaves radiating around a monstrous protome, two crossed shields, one with sea monsters, a breastplate, and a circular shield from behind which project a spear point, helmet and two catapults. It dates from the first century AD.

The same wall has a particularly interesting small funerary *ara* with inscriptions placed at different times on its two faces, referring to different individuals who lived in the second and third centuries AD. At the sides are the two sacred symbols of the *urceus* and the patera. In the last room are some admirable fragments of sarcophagi and funerary reliefs, including the front of a sarcophagus with fluting and pillars dedicated, as appears by the inscription, to Aurelia Macariane by her husband Aurelius Inachulus. It dates from the third century AD. The corner tower contains a selection of materials found in excavations in the complex between 1977 and 1999.

96. Double funerary urn.

97. Sarcophagus with inscription.

The showcase displays coins from imperial, mediaeval and modern times and medieval and Renaissance ceramic tableware. There is a coin (64-66 AD) bearing the likeness of Nero on the obverse and on the reverse the emperor on horseback flanked by a second horseman. Another coin from after 141 AD represents Faustina, wife of Antoninus Pius, on the obverse and on the reverse the figure of Aeternitas, one of the values personified by Faustina at her apotheosis. The two coins were found during excavation of the castle in 1998–1999.

The hoard of sixteen bronze coins from the early fourth century AD was discovered during excavation of a tomb in the palace courtyard. The ceramics were found in excavations in the interior of the palace in 1997–1999. They exemplify developments in pottery in Rome and Latium and contacts with workshops in the centre-north of Italy between the late thirteenth century and the end of the fifteenth.

The fourteenth-century items are a majolica bowl decorated with stylised blue vegetable motifs, a fragment of a jug with a female protome in relief, majolica ware from Orvieto, and a Roman majolica jug decorated with a figure of the *agnus Dei* kind. The fragment of a majolica bowl with stylised blue vegetable motifs is Roman work

98. Relief with a trophy.

from the early fifteenth century. From upper Latium comes a majolica jug decorated with a stylised animal, perhaps a rabbit, and vegetable and geometric reliefs from the earlier fifteenth century.

From the late fifteenth or early sixteenth century comes the majolica ware decorated with flame motifs, and a dish with a flared rim and the arms of the Colonna family in the middle, and a second dish with the arms of the Cybo family. Dishes like these, bearing the arms of patrician families, were distributed to the peasants and others in their service.

On the walls are three fragments of a funerary relief with gladiatorial scenes, one with an inscription, found in 1977 during excavation of the summit of the mausoleum. They probably come from the funerary monument of a person who organised and presented gladiatorial spectacles. Palaeographic and stylistic factors suggest a date from the late third and early fourth century AD.

The excavations of 1998-1999 produced two fragments of red porphyry sculpture, perhaps from a statue of a draped figure from late imperial times, and part of a garland of flowers and fruit from the frieze on the mausoleum. (C.D.S.)

99. Sestertius of Faustina Maggiore, reverse with personification of Aeternitas.

100. Sestertius of Nero, obverse with the head of the emperor.

101. *Pottery jug from Latium.*

102. *Fragment of a jug with a female protome.*

103. *Fragment of a bowl of Roman workmanship.*

104. *Plate with the arms of the Colonna.*

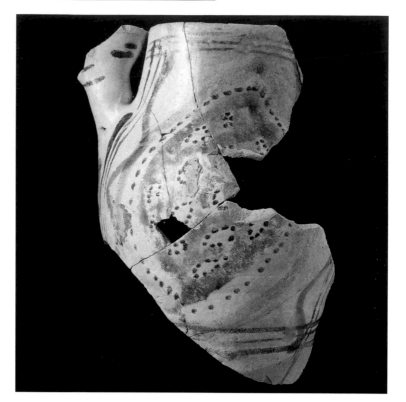

84

105. *"The clamps
of Vitruvius." Builders'
clamps for raising blocks
of stone in an etching
by G.B. Piranesi
(Le Antichità Romane,
III, LIV, 167, 1756)*

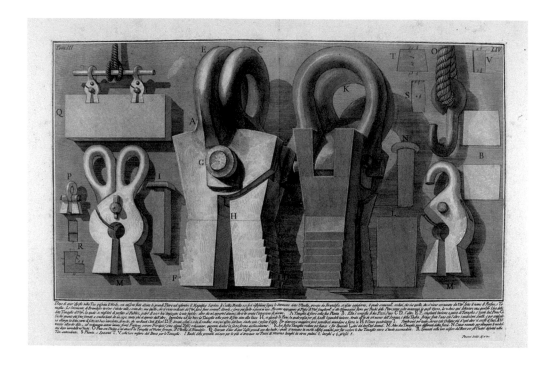

BUILDING MATERIALS AND TECHNIQUES USED IN THE MAUSOLEUM OF CECILIA METELLA AND THE CASTRUM CAETANI

The Roman Tomb

Architecture in the ancient world was always closely conditioned by the materials locally available and these in turn had a strong influence on the invention and development of building techniques, at times even helping to develop their potential. The ideals in a building, according to Vitruvius, who wrote ten books on architecture in the later first century BC, were: *firmitas*, the solidity and stability of the structure; *utilitas*, the convenient arrangement of parts; and *venustas*, the beauty and elegance of the whole. Of course the choice of materials was also influenced by the taste of the period, the preferences and means of the client, the purpose and size of the building; while the techniques adopted were dependent on the skill and knowledge of the builders. The outcome called for a perfect combination between the quality of the materials employed and skill in the various phases of construction.

Opus Caementicium

The Romans' need to find materials and techniques enabling them to build very tall structures led from the third century BC to the development of *opus caementicium*, also called *structura caementorum*. This technique took its name from *caementa*, fragments of stone of various kinds, shapes and forms, bound together by mortar to form a compound of outstanding hardness and durability: concrete. The introduction of concrete transformed the structure of walls and the way they were built. The new material was used alone in the foundations or elevations of small buildings but more often formed an inner shell in walls then faced with stonework of various kinds, from *opus quadratum* to brick. It was, in fact the spread of concrete that led to the appearance of these different facing techniques. The builders worked in stages, erecting two external facing walls of various kinds of masonry (bricks, blocks of stone, rubble etc.) which formed a mould and then they filled the space with fresh concrete. They waited for the first layer to set before continuing upward. The ingredients might be first mixed and then cast or the *caementa* might be pressed into fairly liquid mortar. The mortar was generally a mixture of lime and pozzolana or lime and sand.

This technique revolutionised Roman architecture, which became distinguished for the creation of colossal structures that are still impressive—theatres, aqueducts, baths—and for the bold use of archi-

106. Opus
caementicum *in the
plinth of the tomb.*

tectural forms to roof over huge spaces, especially the arch and vault.
The use of *opus caementicium* is exemplified in the core of the plinth
of the mausoleum.

Opus Quadratum

Also known as *etrusca disciplina* and *saxum quadratum*, this was one
of the most ancient and widespread techniques in the whole Mediterranean area, especially where there was plenty of stone that could be
hewn easily (tufa, limestone). In Rome its use is recorded from the
archaic period (late seventh-early sixth century BC).
It consisted of laying squared stones in horizontal courses; the bond
might be homogeneous (with blocks placed all head-on or edge-on),
a feature of Greek work, or with blocks or rows laid alternately head-
on and edge-on, typical of the city of Rome. The stone wall might be
smooth or finished as different kinds of ashlar work, at times emphasised by *anathyrosis*, a smooth band of stonework, varying in
width, whose function was not only aesthetic—to set off the workmanship—but also practical, as a way of filling in fissures between
blocks.
No mortar was used between the blocks of stone, which were laid one
on top of the other and held in place by fastenings that were either
set horizontally (cramps) or vertically (pins). The cramps were made
of wood, iron, bronze or lead, and the shape varied: rectangular, a
double swallowtail, the form of the Greek letter π or a double-T. The
perishability of wood and the habit of scavenging metals means that
few of these cramps survive but grooves cut into the stones to hold
them are often visible.
The stones were rough-hewn and their surfaces dressed in the quarry; they would be finished on the building site, sometimes after
they were laid in the wall. This was done in stages, starting at the
bottom, and complicated tackle was needed to hoist them into
place. The use of this equipment is attested not only by the obvi-
ous difficulty presented by some structures but also by marks left by

107. Opus quadratum
in the facing of the tomb.

the different kinds of tackle on the stones.

After the introduction of concrete in the third century BC, *opus quadratum*, until then commonly used, was restricted to the parts of the building which required greater stability or as a facing material firmly anchored to the concrete core.

Opus quadratum was used to face the cylinder of the tomb and its plinth, though in the latter it is poorly preserved.

Opus Testaceum

The most successful technique for facing the concrete core was called *opus testaceum* and based on the use of flat bricks fired in a furnace. It rapidly spread throughout the Roman world. The earliest examples, from Julian and Augustan times, employed fragments of house tiles for facing walls exposed to damp, such as the cells of some sepulchres. Under Tiberius (14–37 AD) it was used systematically. Bricks split into triangles were used so that they would bond better with the conglomerate. They were laid by hand, with each piece gently pressed into the mortar while leaving the cut edge of the brick, sometimes ground smooth, on the outside. Some examples are so carefully laid that they seem to have been ground smooth, dry or with water, when the facing was complete.

In the case of structures subject to very heavy weights, smooth brickwork running the whole thickness of the wall replaced the usual technique of the two outer curtains with a concrete core.

At times the mortar between the joints was finished by using the edge of the trowel to draw a horizontal line in it, and smoothed to provide an even surface. At times more refined kinds of mortar were used to bring out decorative features of the brick facade, which might be enlivened by portals, string courses or tympana made of brickwork or by using brickwork of two colours to form simple patterns.

Opus testaceum appears in the facing of the cell and to some extent on the upper corridor of the mausoleum.

108. Opus quadratum
in the facing of the wall
of the cell of the tomb.

109. Brick conglomerate
in the floor of the cell
of the tomb.

Brick Conglomerate

This material incorporated brick dust mixed with lime and sand or pozzolana in order to create a material with excellent powers of waterproofing.

The Romans had no precise term for it; in the literature it is indicated by general or descriptive terms. The brick and the pozzolana, when the latter was used, made it impermeable. A thin layer was used to face walls or poured as a solid mass in the floors of interiors exposed to moisture inside or outside. It was commonly used in swimming pools, *suspensurae* (floors protecting the cavities under heated rooms), or as a

protective facing of vaults and terraces. This conglomerate is visible in the floor of the cell of the tomb.

Flint

Flint (in Latin *silex* or *lapis durus*) was widely used in the Roman world. Its hardness and durability made it especially suitable for paving roads. It was cut into large polygonal flagstones set flush with each other. Also commonly used were flakes of flint set on edge in the cement conglomerate, above all in foundations, and as small pyramidal blocks in the facing of *opus reticulatum*.

Flint is a stone of volcanic formation, geologically a siliceous (*leucitic*) lava. The flint used by the Romans was produced by the eruptive phase of the volcanoes of Latium in the Alban hills. The lava beds extended across the Roman countryside from Marino as far as the tomb of Cecilia Metella. There were numerous quarries in the side of the beds, one of which was revealed by excavations of the interior of the Caetani castle.

Lime

Produced around the Mediterranean as the result of firing stone from at least the fifth century BC, lime (in Latin *calx*) was used in Rome as the principal component of mortar. Limestone, mostly calcium carbonate, was fired by skilled workers in special furnaces. The anhydrous carbon was released and the oxide of lime, or quicklime (*calx viva*), was left. The quicklime was "slaked" by putting it in great troughs of water, in which the temperature rapidly rose to about 300° C. Part of the water evaporated while the lime absorbed the rest and became pulverised, in which form it was called slaked lime (*calx extincta*). Adding water to slaked lime produced *calx macerata*.

Sand

Called *harena* or *sabulum*, sand was one of the materials the Romans used to make mortar. It is a hard, fine, granular material derived from the crumbling of various rocks, generally with a high siliceous content.

Sand extracted from sandpits, river beds or the seashore was used provided it contained no soil. For this reason when greater solidity was essential, the sand was generally washed and used only when dry.

Pozzolana

The use of pozzolana enabled mortar to set even in contact with water. However the Romans used it also as a more effective binding material to increase resistance to frost during construction. Pozzolana rapidly absorbs the moisture in the lime, making walls exceptionally solid and compact.

The Latin name, *pulvis puteolanus*, comes from the city of Puteoli, now Pozzuoli, where beds in the area of the Phlegraean Fields as well as in the Roman Campania provided the best material.

It is a compound of volcanic origin erupted in the form of *lapilli* (fine stony particles) which in contact with the air are deposited in more or less compact beds. Its binding properties depend on the age of the bed. In ancient times it was usually extracted by sinking shafts, as shown by many tunnels in the suburbs of Rome.

Travertine

From its earliest use in the late second century travertine (*lapis tiburtina*) was the stone most widely used in Rome for very large buildings, especially outer walls or the facades. Its major use in architecture was as *opus quadratum*, but flakes or odd pieces were used to make lime or provide rubble for conglomerate. It is a sedimentary limestone resulting from the deposition of calcareous substances in the waters of the River Aniene. The main quarries in ancient times were at the Acque Albule of Tivoli, where modern workings have effaced all the signs of the ancient workings. It is a porous limestone stratified horizontally and containing cavities of various sizes created by the pieces of vegetable and animal matter incorporated in the sediments.

Brick

Roman fired bricks, called *testae* or *lateres cocti*, were made out of a mixture of clay and water to which was often added a small quantity of straw or sand or fine pozzolana. The mixture was poured into square moulds of standard sizes to produce three kinds of brick: *bessales*, two thirds of a Roman foot square (c. 20 centimetres), *sesquipedales*, one and a half Roman feet square (c. 45 centimetres), and *bipedales*, two Roman feet square (c. 60 centimetres). Though the square shape made it necessary to cut the flat bricks into triangles before use, it was adopted for ease of transport and to limit deformation during drying. The bricks were dried first in the sun and then under cover in a ventilated space. A certain number of bricks were stamped to make the tally of production easier. Only later were they fired in furnaces at 800° C. The different kinds of brick, used for different purposes, depended on the firing and the combination of ingredients.

In the Mediaeval Complex

Building techniques in the Middle Ages varied greatly because of local differences. At Rome the principal factor was the very large number of ancient monuments, which suggested building techniques and afforded materials which could be reused in new buildings; the local workmen also inherited building traditions in an unbroken continuity between late antiquity and the Middle Ages. Then the choice of techniques, materials and detailing was often bound up with the specific purpose of different constructions, differentiating those with aesthetic or representative functions from fortifications, dwellings or outhouses.

Opera Saracinesca

This masonry was made up of horizontal courses of blocks of squared tufa, varying in thickness from six to eight centimetres, laid in beds of mortar two or three centimetres thick. The name reflects the belief current in the nineteenth century that it was introduced to Italy during the Saracen invasions of the ninth century. Scholars now date its development to the twelfth–thirteenth centuries, with some works from the fourteenth. It is unconnected with the Saracens.

The use of bocks of tufa (*tufelli*) was common in simpler forms of housing, now rarely preserved, and in restoring, strengthening or building onto earlier structures, especially churches and basilicas. We have much information about the use of tufa in tower-houses, a very common kind of urban residence erected by patrician families; tufa was used because it was light and well suited to tall buildings. The purpose of the building did not determine the building technique but rather the quality of the material. Various kinds of tufa were used, varying in colour, texture and porosity, taken from quarries or stripped from the old Roman buildings. The softer, more friable kinds were generally used in larger blocks, rough hewn and less carefully finished. But in most cases *opera saracinesca* seems fairly refined work with the stones carefully cut and dressed, and were sometimes given a finish of mortar. In this last respect the systems of finishing the stones were a development of Roman building techniques: mortar might be dabbed or smoothed onto the stones; sometimes it was used to imitate a false curtain wall of stonework: a fine layer of rendering was spread over the wall and then the edge of the trowel or dark paint was used to imitate very regular stonework. At times horizontal courses of brick were laid at intervals in the stonework to keep it regular.

Opera saracinesca is recorded above all in the area under the influence of Rome and the great Roman families.

It can be seen in the battlemented upper work of the tomb, in Palazzo Caetani and the church of San Nicola.

110. Opera saracinesca

Muratura a Selcetti

A building technique regarded as contemporary with *opera saraci-nesca* (twelfth–fourteenth centuries), but less elegant and refined, is termed *muratura a selcetti*. This is masonry made of small, irregular fragments of stone of various kinds roughly cut and laid in courses with plenty of mortar to compensate for the irregularity of the stones and keep the courses level. This technique served to reuse old building materials available locally. The commonest material was flint scavenged from the old Roman roads, hence the name used in the archaeological literature. In addition to flint large quantities of marble fragments were also used and, to a lesser degree, tufa, *peperino* and brick. No attempt was generally made to sort them but at times courses of flint were alternated with bands of marble or other materials for decorative effect.

This technique was not only contemporary with *opera saracinesca* but also employed fairly small pieces of stone and is found at Rome and in areas dominated by the leading Roman families. It appears in the *castrum Caetani*, though much altered by later restoration.

111. Flintstones in the wall of the castrum

Brickwork

At Rome from Augustan times bricks fired in furnaces were the commonest form of facing for walls and the Middle Ages perpetuated this ancient technique. The material erected between the fifth and fifteenth centuries generally came from earlier buildings; a revival of brick-making under Theodoric in the fifth and sixth centuries was short-lived. Only in the later fifteenth century, under the influence of Lombard builders, did brick-making revive at Rome.

The habit of reusing materials from old buildings did not, however, compromise the aesthetic quality of the architecture. The skills of the workmen often made up for irregularities in the form, colour, and size of the bricks. While some walls are very roughly built, with the bricks laid in undulating courses (especially in work of the eighth and ninth centuries), others are so carefully laid that it is hard to distinguish the scavenged materials in carefully finished walls, dabbed, smoothed or faced to imitate regular masonry. Reused bricks might be sorted into "firsts," used whole or split in half, or "seconds," broken into small pieces. The choice depended on the kind of building and the funds available.

This kind of brickwork can be seen in the great arches of the courtyard and the window embrasures of Palazzo Caetani, in the half-dome of the apse, in window embrasures and the oculus of San Nicola. Occasional rows of bricks were used in the tufa walls of the palace.

Peperino

Peperino, called *lapis albanus* by the Romans, was introduced to Rome in the middle of the republican period (about the fourth century BC) and was used all through imperial times. In the Middle Ages it was rare because the cost of transport from the distant quarries meant only a wealthy client could afford it.

It is easily worked, in blocks of various sizes, or as thin slabs. This explains its use not only in building but also in architectural ornament and sculpture. It survives in columns, architraves, sarcophagi, altars, cippi and inscriptions.

It is a lithoid tufa, very compact, formed by very fine-grained grey volcanic ash. The quarries, still in use a few years ago, are near the railway station at Marino. (C.D.S.)

112. Brickwork.

113. *Face of the quarry
inside Palazzo Caetani.*

GEOLOGY AND SETTLEMENTS. THE SIGNS OF MAN

114. The Vulcano Laziale. *Drawing by D. Mantero.*

The monumental complex of the tomb of Cecilia Metella and the *castrum Caetani* stand on a vast volcanic shield traversed to the north-east by the Statuario-Caffarella-Acquataccio-Almone depression and to the south-west by Tor Carbone-Grotta Perfetta depression. A distinctive feature of the site of the complex is the edge of the lava beds of Capo di Bove, part of the volcanic formations created by the Vulcano Laziale, the mountain system of the Alban hills, a dominant feature of the landscape in the countryside south of Rome.

The lava bed of Capo di Bove, first identified in the early eighteenth century close to the tomb, is named after the estate traversed by the last part of the lava flow; the estate in turn takes its name from the ox-skulls in the frieze of the tomb of Cecilia Metella.

The lava, also called "Cecilite" after the tomb, has always attracted the interest of scholars because it is the closest to the city and the Appian Way runs above it. It is a siliceous lava produced during an eruptive phase of the Vulcano Laziale called the phase of Faete or of the Fields of Hannibal, dated to the Middle Pleistocene (260,000 years ago). Its course was determined by the earlier conformation of the land. Varying in thickness from 6 to 12 metres it extends over

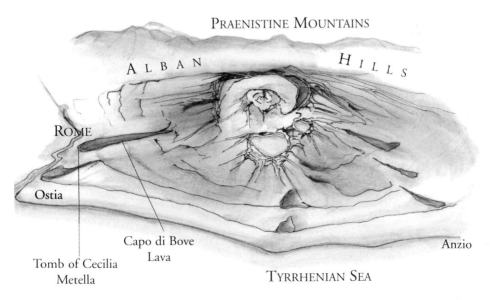

PRAENISTINE MOUNTAINS

ALBAN HILLS

ROME

Ostia

Capo di Bove Lava

Tomb of Cecilia Metella

Anzio

TYRRHENIAN SEA

115. Effects of differentiated erosion. The lava bed fills the valley bottom; surface water erodes the softer ground at the sides till the lava bed forms a plateau above the countryside. Drawing by D. Mantero.

110 kilometres from Frattocchie di Marino to the tomb of Cecilia Metella. It formed a ridge as the softer ground around it was gradually eroded. Contact between the incandescent lava flow and the underlying beds gave the latter to a distinctive brownish-red colour. The strata below are not visible but have been identified by core-boring. They consist of the eruptive beds named after Villa Senni, dated to about 400,000 years ago, consisting of pozzolana, the tufa of Villa Senni and tawny-coloured tufa.

Since ancient times there have been numerous quarries at the sides of the lava bed. The stone was called *silex* and *lapis durus* or *lapis Tusculanus* by the Romans (now called *selce* or *sercio* by the locals). The lava is compact making it hard to carve and was used only in the form of flagstones, cubes and *sanpietrini* (see below) for paving roads, or in flakes and rubble as *caementa* as in the plinth of the

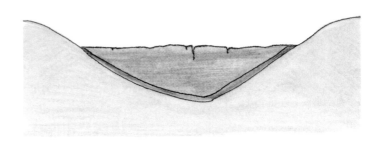

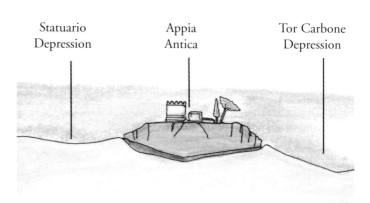

Statuario Depression   Appia Antica   Tor Carbone Depression

The Vulcano Laziale (Alban Hills)

The Vulcano Laziale is a broad mountainous structure consisting of numerous craters formed by explosions and eruptions at various times and rising up to 1000 metres in the countryside south of Rome.

The volcanic activity began about 600,000 years ago and was divided into three main phases, each subdivided into cycles.

The first is the "Tuscolano-Artemisio phase," with an initial eruption that created immense pyroclastic beds often over 90 metres thick above the earlier formations (and filled in valleys, lake and river beds) in the eastern sector of the complex, followed by the lava flow of Acquacetosa. The material emitted in the next cycle spread to distances of almost 100 kilometres. This created the immense deposits of red pozzolana and Vallerano black pozzolana. The last cycle (c. 360,000 years ago) produced the Villa Senni stratum (superior pozzolana or pozzolanella, a lithoidal or tawny tufa, and the tufa of Villa Senni).

The second phase is known as the phase of Faete or of the Fields of Hannibal, from the locality of the same name between the centre of Rocca di Papa and the Pratoni del Vivaro. Dating from 300,000 to 200,000 years ago it consisted of explosive activity of the "Stromboli" type with eruption of detritus interspersed with local lava flows (lava of Capo di Bove).

The third or final hydromagmatic phase came between 200,000 and c. 25,000–20,000 years ago; it consisted of freato-magmatic eruptions caused by the sudden contact between water and the seething magma. The violent ex-plosion that ensued formed a vertical column of vapour with a dense ring-shaped cloud at its base (called a "base surge"), moving at a speed of over 100 km/h. This activity took place in the western sector and the craters can still be distinguished, some of them forming lakes (Albano, Nemi, Ariccia). A distinctive feature of the Alban hills is a vast plateau sloping gently to the Tyrrhenian Sea, while to the north and east the terrain is more rugged because of erosion by waterways forming gorges like those of the "Etruscan" land-scape of Upper Latium. The surface hydrography follows a radial arrangement and cuts into the slopes of the mountain chain.

General stratigraphic scheme of the eruptive phases of the Vulcano Laziale (Alban hills). Drawing by D. Mantero.

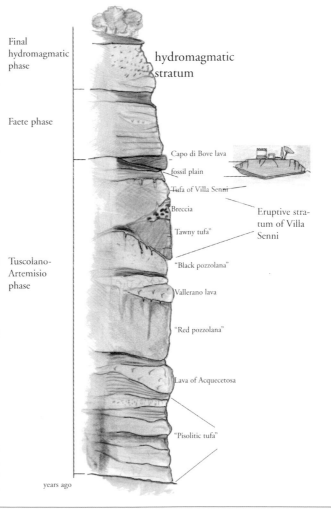

Final hydromagmatic phase

hydromagmatic stratum

Faete phase

Capo di Bove lava

fossil plain

Tufa of Villa Senni

Breccia

Tawny tufa"

Eruptive stratum of Villa Senni

"Black pozzolana"

Tuscolano-Artemisio phase

Vallerano lava

"Red pozzolana"

Lava of Acquecetosa

"Pisolitic tufa"

years ago

116. View from the
palace courtyard.
In the foreground
the face of the quarry
and the reddish fossil
plain; to the left
the tomb and at the end
on the right the shaft.
Photo by P. Procaccini.

tomb (revealed by diffractometric tests on a number of lava sam-
ples). The historian Livy recounts that in 189 BC the Appian Way
was repaved with flint; the earlier paving was *saxo quadrato* (perhaps
of *peperino*). The information is useful because it tells us when tufa was replaced by flint in the paving of roads.

It should be noted that *sanpietrini*, stone blocks in the form of a
truncated pyramid with a square base, commonly called *selci* or
quadrucci according to the size and sometimes "cubes of porphyry,"
have been used for paving streets in Rome only since the eighteenth
century.

Excavations at Palazzo Caetani have revealed that there was a single
quarry working the lava beds and it was definitely active when the
tomb was built.

The underlying formation of Villa Senni, about 4 metres below the foundations of Palazzo Caetani, contain tunnels belonging to a pozzolana quarry from Roman times, perhaps a prelude to the quarrying of the lava beds above. The pozzolana was mixed with mortar and used in the walls of the monument.

The mediaeval builder of the palace must have known about this quarry. A vertical shaft inside the castle leads into the tunnels and is still visible. The tunnels have been explored using speleological, geophysical and microgravimetric techniques and core-boring supplemented by filming. (R.M., R.S.)

117. Stratigraphic diagram of the complex of the tomb and Palazzo Caetani.
Drawing by D. Mantero.

Techniques of extracting lava and pozzolana

The close connection between the monumental complex, the Appian Way and the local rocks enables us to understand how the Romans exploited their mineral resources.

Inside the palace there are clear signs that the lava beds have been hewn into, both to quarry material and prepare the site for the construction of the tomb.

This was an open quarry, with cutting proceeding by stages down to the base of the bed and into the vertical rock face. Since the lava is very compact and difficult to carve with a chisel, mallets were used to hammer wedges into the strata and natural fissures of the rock, which was then prised out; or picks were used to hew out blocks of the desired shape and size.

Inside Palazzo Caetani there are furrows which were probably made by cartwheels or runners of the sledges used to transport the stone. Pozzolana was extracted by cutting out underground chambers joined by tunnels and supported by pillars according to a very precise set of rules. At times the rules were ignored, especially when the mine was derelict: pillars might be hewn away and the tunnels deepened, causing falls.

When the workings were abandoned the underground chambers were often adapted to use as depositories, shelters, and even mushroom farms in modern times.

Cutting the lava using wedges and a mallet.
Drawing by D. Mantero.

*118. "Blocks" in a bank
of lava.*

Bibliography

G.B. Piranesi, *Le Antichità Romane*, II, III, Rome 1756.
L. Canina, *La prima parte della via Appia dalla Porta Capena a Bovillae...*, Roma 1853.
G. Digard, *Le domaine des Gaetani au tombeau de Cecilia Metella, Mélanges G.B. Rossi, Recueil de traveaux publiés par l'Ecole Française*, 1892, pp. 281–290, cols. 913–926.
F. Azzurri, *Osservazioni sul fregio marmoreo del sepolcro di Cecilia Metella*, BCom, 23, 1895, pp. 14–25.
R. Lanciani, *Storia degli scavi di Roma*, 1902–1912, I, pp. 37, 59, IV, p. 123.
A. Muñoz, *La Tomba di Cecilia Metella*, BCom, 41, 1913, pp. 4–14.
P.A. Frutaz, *Le carte del Lazio*, Rome 1972.
G. Tomassetti, *La campagna Romana antica medioevale e moderna*, Florence 1910, updated edition L. Chiumenti, F. Bilancia, Florence 1975, pp. 101–114.
R. Cereghino, *Tomba di Cecilia Metella. Saggio di scavo all'interno del Castello Caetani*, BCom, 91, 1986, pp. 605–607.
P. Meogrossi, *Tomba di Cecilia Metella. Restauri e indagini nell'area del Castello Caetani*, BCom, 91, 1986, pp. 601–605.
P. Zanker, *Augusto e il potere delle immagini*, Turin 1989, pp. 19–21, 81, 309.
H. von Hesberg, *Monumenta.*

I sepolcri romani e la loro architettura, Rome 1992, pp. 9, 18, 40, 44, 45, 47, 116, 239, 264.
R. Paris, "Il mausoleo di Cecilia Metella e il castrum Caetani sulla via Appia," in *Via Appia. Sulle ruine della magnificenza antica*, exhibition catalogue, Rome 1997, pp. 53–54.
F. Rausa, *Pirro Ligorio. Tombe e mausolei dei romani*, Rome 1997, pp. 43–51.
A. Ambrogi, *Il sarcofago cosiddetto di Cecilia Metella: ambito produttivo e cronologico*, Xenia VI, 1997, pp. 39–80.

For Mediaeval Aspects

F. Borgnana, *Del castello e della chiesa de' Caetani nella Via Appia*, Rome 1866.
M. Righetti Tosti-Croce, *Un'ipotesi per Roma angioina: la cappella di S. Nicola nel castello di Capo di Bove: Roma anno 1300*, edited by Angiola Maria Romanini, Rome 1983, pp. 497–512.
A. Cortonesi, *Terra e signori nel Lazio Medioevale. Un'economia rurale nei secoli XIII-XIV*, Naples 1988.
P. Toubert, *Dalla terra ai castelli. Paesaggio, agricoltura e poteri nell'Italia medievale*, Turin 1995.
D. Esposito, *Tecniche costruttive murarie medievali. Murature a tufelli in area romana*, Rome 1997.

F. Allegrezza, *Trasformazioni della nobiltà medievale nel Trecento: Roma Medievale. Aggiornamenti*, edited by P. Delogu, Florence 1998, pp. 211–220.
Castelli del Lazio meridionale, edited by G. Giammaria, Bari 1998.

For Geological Aspects

A.G. Segre, *Note illustrative alla carta geologica d'Italia Foglio 150 Roma*, Roma, Servizio Geologico, 1967.
U. Ventriglia, *La geologia della città di Roma*, Amministrazione Provinciale di Roma, Rome 1971.
D. De Rita, C. Rosa, *Definizione della stratigrafia e della geocronologia di alcune effusioni laviche nell'area dei Colli Albani (Lava dell'Acqua Acetosa e Lava di Vallerano)*, Rendiconti della Società Geologica Italiana, 13, 1990, pp. 143–146.

Scientific Director
Rita Paris

Director of Works
Piero Meogrossi

Works Contractor
ISARM

Archaeological Assistance at the Excavations
Carla De Stefanis
Paola Procaccini

Exhibition Design
Carla De Stefanis
Rita Paris

Technical Assistance
Livia Giammichele

Structural and Design Consultant
Salvatore D'Agostino
with Mariangela Bellomo

Geological Consultants
Soc. ALTA, DGRilievi, Gruppo speleologico CAI, Servizio Geologico Nazionale
Coordination: Laboratorio geologico-cartografico e di aerofotointerpretazione della SAR,
with the collaboration of Francesca Cortignani, Diego Mantero, Roberto Ricci.
Technical and Engineering Assistance:
Sergio Di Maio (Sering)

Environmental Consultant
Massimo De Vico

Restoration of Works
Cooperativa Opera, Clima Restauri, CEFME; Laboratorio restauro della SAR;
Department of Metal Works and Ancient Weapons; Ceramics and Glass Department;
Department of Stone Tablets; Technical Direction and Coordination:
Giovanna Bandini

Display Material
MCM s.r.l.
Realisation of the Marble Plan:
Fratelli De Tomassi

Display Cases
Green Allestimenti

Ticket Office
Progetto Andrea Vidotto
Realizzazione TMF

Reliefs
Massimo Chimenti
Germano Foglia
Maria Naccarato

Photographs
Stefano Castellani

Photograph and Archive Research
Patrizia Cavalieri
Carla De Stefanis
Federico Rausa

Thanks go to
Marilena Mulas (Archivio SAR); Marina Bertinetti, consultant for the inscriptions; Giovanna Bandini, ceramics consultant; Alessandra Melucco Vaccaro, for her advice and suggestions.

This volume was printed on behalf of Elemond S.p.A.
at Mondadori Printing S.p.A.,
Via Castellana 98, Martellago (Venice) in the year 2000